INSPIRED HIGH-END
INTERIOR DESIGN

SHANE REILLY

Schiffer Publishing Ltd

4880 Lower Valley Road, Atglen, PA 19310 USA

Phone: 44 (0) 20 8392-8585; Fax: 44 (0) 20 8392-9876
E-mail: info@bushwoodbooks.co.uk
Website: www.bushwoodbooks.co.uk
Free postage in the U.K., Europe; air mail at cost.Published by Schiffer Publishing Ltd.
4880 Lower Valley Road
Atglen, PA 19310
Phone: (610) 593-1777; Fax: (610) 593-2002
E-mail: Info@schifferbooks.com

For the largest selection of fine reference books on this and related subjects, please visit our web site at
www.schifferbooks.com
We are always looking for people to write books on new and related subjects. If you have an idea for a book please contact us at
the above address.

This book may be purchased from the publisher.
Include $3.95 for shipping.
Please try your bookstore first.
You may write for a free catalog.

In Europe, Schiffer books are distributed by
Bushwood Books
6 Marksbury Ave.
Kew Gardens
Surrey TW9 4JF England

Library of Congress Cataloging-in-Publication Data

Reilly, Shane.
 Inspired high-end interior design / Shane Reilly.
   p. cm.
 ISBN 0-7643-2499-3 (hardcover)
 1. Interior design—Themes, motives. 2. Interior decoration—History—21st century. 1. Title.

NK1990.R45 2006

747—dc22   2006019879

Covers and book designed by: Bruce Waters
Type set in Avant Garde/Humanist 521 BT

ISBN: 0-7643-2499-3
Printed in China

Front Cover credits: 2Michaels Design (Photography by Frank Veteran), Tucker & Marks, Inc. (Photography by Tim Street-Porter), Shane Reilly Inc. (Photography by Margot Hartford), Robert Passal Inc. (Photography by Dennis Krukonski), SKB Architecture and Design (Photography by Gordon Beall), Clodagh (Photography by Daniel Aubry), Edward Lobrano Interior Design Inc. (Photography by Eric Piasecki).

Back Cover: The Jeffrey Design Group (Photography by Mick Hales), Eric Cohler Design (Photography by Francis Smith), DeSousa Hughes (Photography by David Duncan Livingston), Jeffers Design Group(Photography by Cesar Rubio)

ACKNOWLEDGMENTS

Thank you to the family, friends, and clients who have supported my passion for interior design.

Speical thanks to Julie Terrell and Melissa Weyrick, for their assistance with this book.

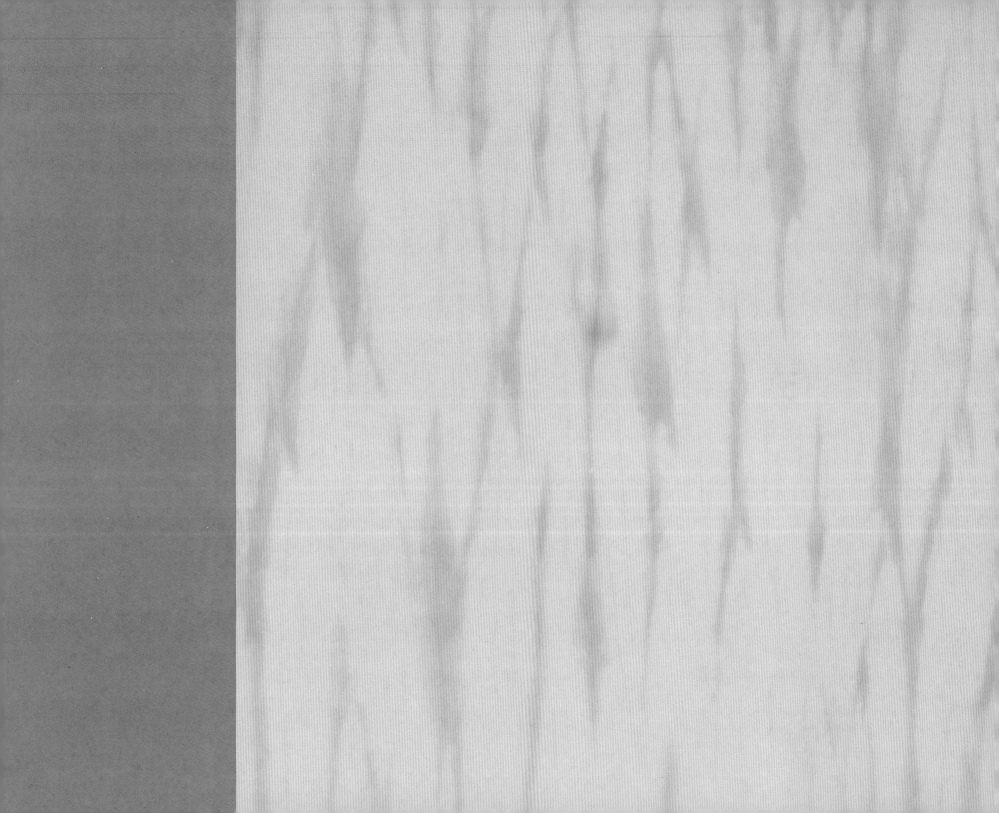

CONTENTS

INTRODUCTION

"High-end design" describes interior design of top quality. High-end design requires furniture, art, and accessories made with superb craftsmanship, timeless beauty, sensual comfort, and visual interest. It demands a designer possessing both creative courage and a disciplined attention to the laws of composition. Most often, high-end design requires both a sizeable budget and a willing client.

High-end interior design is an art; designers must carefully balance color, light, scale, and detail in a three dimensional world. Like painters and sculptors, interior designers operate from an inspiration or idea that helps them select and edit appropriate elements for a composition. The inspiration may come from a color, a piece of art or fabric, a characteristic or emotion, or even the architecture of the space itself.

This book offers the unique opportunity to hear high-end designers say in their own words what inspired them and how they executed on their inspiration. This book is not a how-to book or a resource guide; it is a celebration of high-end design and the designers and architects responsible for creating high-end spaces.

"There is no reason today for people without a lot of money not to live well. I think these retailers today are doing great stuff. But it is not high-end... it is great for someone on a budget. Everyone doesn't have a million dollars to spend decorating an apartment. Today you can have a really cute apartment without spending a lot of money on it."
— Ed Lobrano

"I think high-end design is about being tailor made to a client's needs, taking in the taste and needs along with functionality of a space and providing clients with best furniture - fabrics - antiques - art that is available to create the perfect design for each client's individual taste."
— John Barman

"Nothing connotes the high-end more than something handmade." — Jamie Drake

"Sophisticated does not have to jump out at you and suggest how much money you spent, but the closer you look, the more detail and the level of nuance you see." — Paul Wiseman

"High-end design is a lot of work." — Ernest De la Torre

"High-end design is to commit to the quality of the individual pieces."
— Betty Wasserman

"Real luxury is not having to worry about your home." — Clodagh

"High-end design is more defined by its attention to detail than anything else. A lot of clients don't realize how much works goes into every little thing. If they really want something that is a reflection of them, they have to have patience."
— Kathryn Scott

"The real secret to high-end design is the client, and their ability to appreciate the very best."
— Sherry Hayslip

"High-end design is the ability to incorporate function into quality and correct scale."
— Jay Jeffers

"To custom design your own living spaces in a raw shell is a luxury."
— James Rixner

"Most people think of high-end as expensive, not high quality. I like to think of it as high quality. There are very few people who can do high quality, high-end design."
– Noel Jeffrey

"High-end is what it is—expensive art and furniture."
– Ann Getty

"Unfortunately, today more than ever, design aficionados must confront an increased number of mediocre projects which may have in fact been costly to achieve but lack in the attributes of truly high-end design, as they lack quality in one or more areas of the design agenda."
– Dana Nicholson

"Life shouldn't be about what things cost, it should be about function and beauty, and beauty doesn't have to cost a lot. As long as something is beautiful, I don't care what it costs. One shouldn't predicate purchases based on price."
– Eric Cohler

"High-end is not an accident, it is carefully conceived."
– Maureen Footer

INTRODUCTION CONTINUED

The projects in this book are loosely grouped by the designer's main source of inspiration for the particular project. Each space is shown from several angles, so you feel as if you were walking around the room, or as if you were seeing the space as the designer saw it. Through interviewing the designers about their work, I am able to share with you their design intentions, what they did to execute on their ideas, and why their projects are examples of high-end design. The following is an example of my own work.

SHANE REILLY INC.

When designing the dining room for this spectacular penthouse, I was inspired by the omnipresent cityscape. Floor to ceiling windows framed the sweeping, bright blue sky during the day and sparkly, romantic skyline at night.

Dreaming of sky colors and the glittery view, I created a light, elegant space for entertaining that reflected both an appreciation for luxury and the simple pleasure of a modern aesthetic. To reflect the miles of vertical glass towers outside the window and to provide drama and formality without blocking the view – I selected the room's crown jewel, the Boyd Cascade Divide light fixture. To keep the space from getting too serious or too traditional, I hung colorful, metallic, Jimi Gleason square panels and balanced the stately Altura dining table with sprightly Neidermaier chairs. I reflected the sky's blues and grays in the Stark carpet, cloudy gray Donghia wallpaper, and whimsical, pale blue ceiling.

My design is high-end because of the immense quality of every element in the room and because it succeeded as a composition of color, scale, and texture. The unexpected combination of formal light fixtures and simple, contemporary art provided a bit of visual delight. I chose these pieces because high-end design should not be flat or monotonous; it requires combining pieces in such a way that they create an environment that involves and pleases the viewer.

Photography by Adrian Wilson

"High-end is a room that is very well thought out, organized, refined, with attention to detail making it one harmonious piece."
— Scott Sanders

"Good design transcends money. It takes into consideration what the end user wants."
— Geoff De Sousa

ONE:
ART & COLLECTED OBJECTS

THE WISEMAN GROUP DESIGN, INC.

Inspired by the architecture of this grand Mediterranean manor house in San Francisco, Paul Wiseman wanted to create "a collector's room," fit for a sophisticated, international collector. Wiseman, who believed "it is important to connect place and person," developed a luxurious sitting room appropriate for displaying and enjoying valuable pieces.

Wiseman infused the room with collections of significant value such as contemporary art on the walls, five antique pottery heads, and an antique fabric collection. Three eighteenth century rare silver and silk carpets, together worth over $1 million, covered the floor. The exquisite detail Wiseman added to the room itself made it worthy of a collection. He took a pattern from the Spanish grillwork on the front of the house and had it stenciled on the floor in gold dust. He painted a *trompe l'oeil* crown molding on the ceiling. While there were many examples of valuable antiquities in the room, Wiseman believed "a room has to function well first," so he incorporated several comfortable pieces from Rose Tarlow, including fabulous, custom-made sofas. "You don't want to live in a period room. You can have period things, but you need comfortable upholstery."

Wiseman's approach was to "not miss a single detail." He personally went to Carmel, California, to handpick the driftwood to be displayed in the fireplace so "the color would be just right." The careful selection of every detail and the inherent value of every item is what made this project high-end. "A lot of people do inappropriate things in inappropriate places – it can be very expensive, but very inappropriate. Subtlety is one of the most sophisticated things there is."

Photography by David Duncan Livingston

GLENN GISSLER DESIGN

Glenn Gissler and his wife, Susan Harris, curator and writer of contemporary art, collect modern drawings. They sought to create a space that would best suit their collection of pieces by de Kooning, Richard Tuttle, Kiki Smith, and others. "As drawings are a delicate medium, the palette for the room needed to be very understated – earthy, warm, and no big competing patterns."

Gissler first architecturally corrected the interior of the apartment, balancing it so it "looked like nothing had been done, the space was just pure and perfect." The furnishings he added were either complementary to the artwork or were like artwork themselves. The area rug, a vegetable dye piece from Odegard, provided a soft, organic, neutral background to complement the art. The furniture included a coffee table designed by Edward Wormley for Dunbar, a Donald Judd partner's desk from the 1970s, a pair of French armchairs from the 1930s, and a number of both significant and less significant but beautiful pieces. Gissler chose these items because "they have one foot in history and one foot in the present. They are visually dynamic, graphic, and sculptural, with a modern look, but have age at the same time in terms of finish or shape."

Gissler's design is high-end because it exudes both personal and monetary value. The pieces he collected over years display his refined taste in furniture and knowledge of its history. The art he and his wife have amassed render the living room a place worth spending time in. As Gissler said, "There is no greater luxury than living with art because it gives you a different view of the same world that we look at from our own vision on a daily basis, but we get to see how someone else perceives it. That is luxury."

Photography by Gross & Daley

ZEFF DESIGN

Mark Zeff created a space inspired by the things he needs to be himself. "This room is kind of like the room inside of my brain; it is what I need in my brain for me to work – lots of books, beautiful things, natural and organic – I surround myself with natural inspiration." His living room is a showcase for things he collects. "My home is really about what I find in the world when I travel," and where he has been. Everything in the room has a history to it and a reason why it is there.

Zeff started by creating a dark floor, a design staple of his, and white walls in order to make it simple to display the objects he collects. He said it is "the best way for me to have that parity between what I collect and move around. I can't be stuck with wall paper or a texture." The founding object in the room was an intricate coffee table from Fez. He then designed a simple, square sofa to complement it and flanked it on each side with square blocks of beige ottomans. His two favorite Bibendum chairs by Eileen Gray and a couple of Zeff Design pieces rounded out the main seating area in the room. A French writing table, mounds of books, and collected items make the space a comfortable leisure study for Zeff and his wife. "We use the room as a place to get away from the humdrum of New York City," he said.

Zeff's design is high-end because "everything that is there has a purpose." While the room looks relaxed, in fact, "the books are placed just so; the things on the shelves are placed just so." Zeff believes that "high-end design is the ability to leverage the few pieces in the room."

Photography by Eric Laignel

"If you look at people who have a lot of style, they do not purposefully create style."

ROBERT PASSAL INC.

Robert Passal wanted to make this landing look as if it had "been collected." Passal integrated multiple functions, making the space a great place to have a cocktail, check email, display personal memoirs, or relax on the settee. The variety of activities available and the many items to look at made the area feel "like it had been there forever."

Passal made the room look collected by mixing old and new, modern and traditional pieces. On the lower wall's wainscoting, he used a traditional color; on the upper portion, he used an updated, modern color – a bright tangerine. He combined a 1950s architect's desk with a Venetian chair, and a custom, arts and crafts light fixture, "our take on the antler chandelier," with a Damask on the ceiling. Similarly, he paired a contemporary Lucite console with a variety of art and antiques. Passal integrated bold colors, such as a lavender Warhol, on top of orange walls, next to chartreuse green. "All colors go together, it is just a matter of how you use them." Passal added, "There is a difference between clutter, and having things layered. It is knowing when to stop, knowing how to edit."

Passal's work was high-end because he focused on all the details of the space as integral to the design itself. "Mediocre designers don't focus on details. Good design is a room where the details unravel themselves to you as you experience it."

Photography by Dennis Krukonski

ONE:
ART & COLLECTED OBJECTS

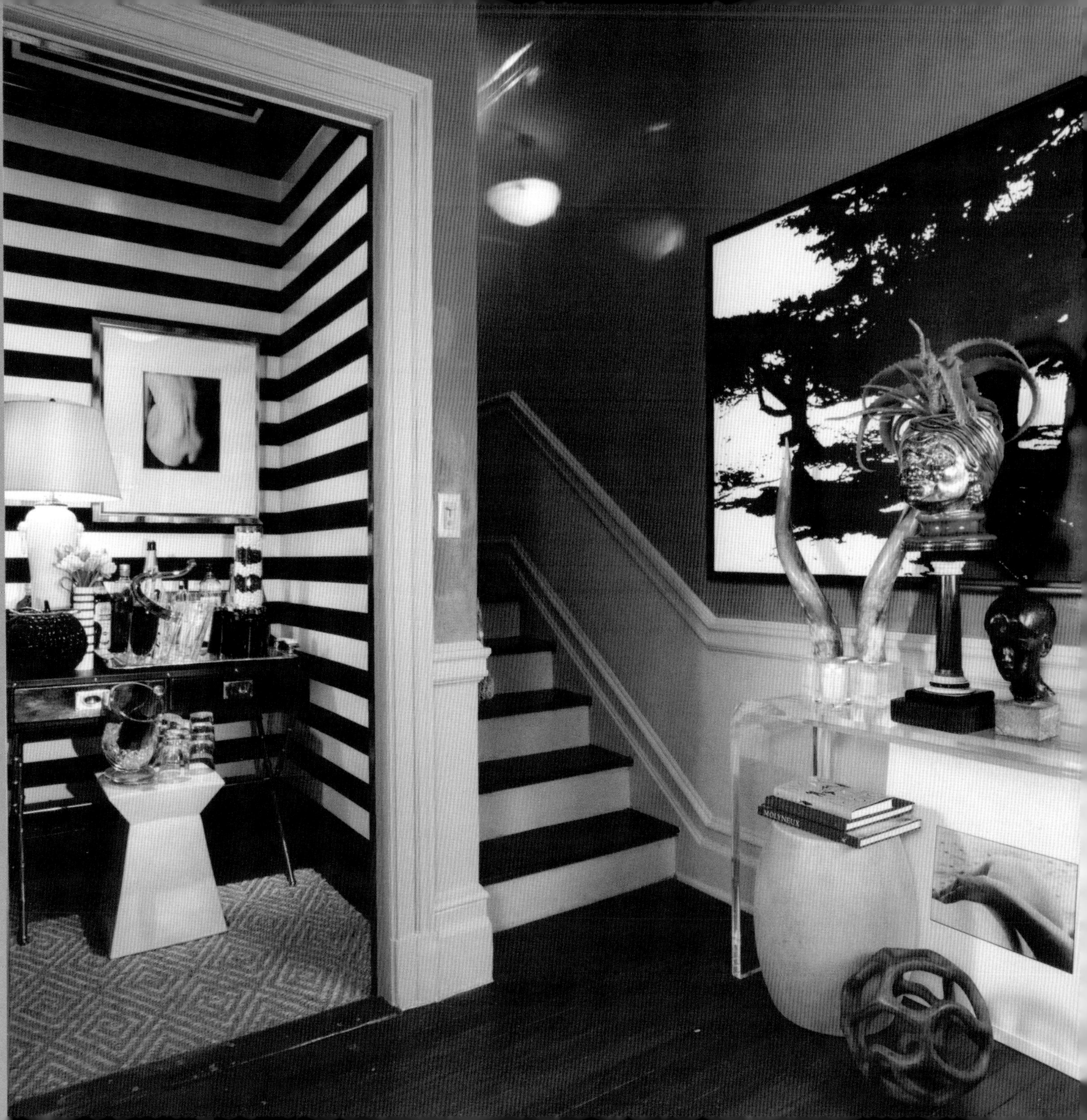

ERIC COHLER DESIGN

Cohler wanted to "create my own little art gallery" in his uptown New York apartment. Cohler said of his work, "When I approach an interior design project, I approach it from a curatorial standpoint." Cohler carefully edits out what pieces do not belong and then adds back in key pieces to make a room come together.

As curator of his own apartment, Cohler recognized that he was short on wall space. As such, he suspended his collection of eighteenth century English portraiture and twentieth century abstract paintings from steel cables in front of his wall of windows. "The room is about the art," he added, "I thought of the furniture as people who would be inside the exhibition looking around." He designed a chocolate brown sofa made with a soft, loose cashmere-mohair by Donghia. The tree pattern rug Cohler designed with Asha Carpet reflected his taste for darker, more muted colors, and it undulates across the room, making it appear wider. He added the red acrylic resin coffee table not only because it provided a slight burst of color, but also because it was inexpensive. "I like to mix the inexpensive with the expensive. I like that polarity. I think in life things can become too expensive, and then they become fragile and brittle and we don't want to touch them or go near them." Similarly, Cohler mixed an inexpensive reproduction white Saarinen table with a couple of valuable antique lamps in the same space.

The space is high-end because of the quality of the art, finishes, and textures. "I like the space to feel sophisticated, world-class, intellectualized, like it was thought through, that it was put together." Cohler suggested a key element to high-end design is to add just the right amount of things, and store others that are not necessary. "You don't want to just add things or it will look like a curiosity shop," he added, "The room works for me, I feel happy every time I go into it."

"It is very hard to differentiate yourself today, and that is what a designer should do."

Photography by Francis Smith

GEOFFREY BRADFIELD INC.

Geoffrey Bradfield understood the importance of this exception-ally large estate on exclusive Further Lane in East Hampton, yet he wanted the space to be "not serious," "not gloomy," "young," and "extremely inviting". Fortunately, the clients contributed valuable artwork by Helen Frankenthaler and Kenneth Noland, which served as the basis for the design of the room. "It is creative to me to work around important art."

The art helped balance the tremendous views outside and define the space inside which otherwise would be "quite cavernous." The room had soaring ceilings and Bradfield did not want it to feel like an airplane hangar, so with the paintings as backdrops he worked with a similar, simple, cheery palette. Paying tribute to the Native American tribes who had lived in the area, Bradfield designed floor lamps after wigwams, complete with lacings in leather. The fireplace emerged as a sculptural element, and the ceiling, wherever oak was showing, was pickled. "It is very edited, refined, but it is very inviting."

Bradfield believed the value of the art and how it was incorpo-rated into this room is what made it high-end. "The quality, although it is subtle, has a very loud voice."

Photography by Durston Saylor

ALAN TANKSLEY, INC.

Alan Tanksley was inspired to make the library for the modern collector. His design called for a calm background for collecting, along with important furniture, accessories, and art.

Taking a cue from the room's wainscoting by keeping everything low, Tanksley aimed to emphasize horizontal lines. Tanksley purposefully designed the room so that it could be used for multiple purposes, including a quiet reprieve or place to enjoy an intimate meal. He worked with Clarence House fabrics, using the company's traditional fabrics in unusual ways. Tanksley did not want the furniture to be "subservient" to the art, so he selected extraordinary pieces that held their own. Some key pieces included a bronze oak commode by French sculptor Ingrid Donat and French 1940s game chairs by Jules Luleu. Tanksley designed an original bookcase wrapped in topstitched, ivory leather, and peppered the room with art and accessories by renowned mid-century designers.

Tanksley's design is high-end because it offers, "a subtly in the details, a tailored sensibility," and simply, "the room is full of valuable art and antiques." Tanksley believed that high-end design comes from "understanding how to approach a room," and the "finesse that comes from the balance of different materials."

Photography by John M. Hall

DE LA TORRE DESIGN STUDIO

Ernest De la Torre focused on the art first. The two paintings by Robert Dash, a contemporary of Jackson Pollack, ignited the room and initiated the color palette. Finding the vintage yellow sofa in its original fabric sealed the direction of the space. He chose the rest of the pieces to fit the client's taste for mid-century furniture, but softened and enriched the look.

De la Torre chose black for the accompanying sofa because "black sets yellow off beautifully," and "yellow and black contrast, which suits the client who likes colors to be well-defined." In the dining area, the hard lines of the room were softened by the richness of the uneven, bamboo table surface and the rounded, white, leather Saarinen chairs. De la Torre added the brown-tinted wall mirror to provide a warm reflection of the space. The luxurious wool drapery fabric by Holland and Sherry is exceptional, and "not a lot of people would spend money on such a thing."

This room is high-end because when you walk in, "The very subtle quality of the pieces gets picked up by the eye." De la Torre makes a lot of his own fabrics and furniture for clients, which he claimed is the "ultimate luxury." "To have a beautiful fabric tailored specifically for you, there is no replacing that."

Photography by Peter Murdock Photography

DARREN HENAULT
INTERIORS, INC.

Darren Henault wanted to restore his apartment's pre-war charm and make it a comfortable, relaxing place. "I want people to walk in and flop down on anything they want to flop on."

Henault achieved his look by sanding and darkening the floors, fixing the moldings, and adding custom panel doors. The Edwin Lutyens light fixture, with its silk-wrapped electrical cords, danced across the ceiling, creating pools of light. To give the space a sense of character and history, Henault designed the sofa, club chair, and banquette based on nineteenth century English designs, but changed the scale of the pieces to make them more comfortable. He covered them in high-end, hearty fabrics that "last like iron." "Everything is beautiful, everything is well thought out, everything is high-end, but not so fussy." Henault did not adhere to structured furniture arrangements, but rather loosely placed pieces. "The apartment is not too precious, I want it to be used, I want people to take their shoes off and hang out."

Henault does not care for most contemporary upholstery, so he focused on collecting and sourcing beautiful individual pieces to fill specific needs. "The design is eclectic, but I don't like the word eclectic because that sounds like flea market – this is more studied than that."

Photography by Wouter Van dur Tol

"I don't like two dimensional rooms that are just a pretty picture and feel cheap every time you touch them. I want my work to be three-dimensional."

MARTHA ANGUS INC.

Martha Angus aspired to create a serene, cheery space for her client who loved important art. Working with a palette of neutral beiges, taupes, and a bit of yellow, Angus designed an elegant living room for her client's good taste and collection of beautiful things. "It is like you are painting, but in a 3D way. The same way a painting is great, a room is great. When it is right, it is not a cerebral, thought out thing – it just works. And you know."

Angus included antique Dufour panels behind the sofa "because they have a handmade quality to them, and they almost provide another window." Angus added further richness to the room with throw pillows made with antique fabrics by Cora Ginsburg. The Aubusson carpet, a pair of Jean Michel Frank boxy, taupe-colored loveseats, and a Rose Tarlow club chair with Fortuny fabric rounded out the room. The two books on the coffee table are carved from white marble; Angus added them to "counter-balance something old with something new." Angus carried yellow around the room with the client's contemporary, yellow painting, a bright blaze of yellow damask in the window, and the flowers next to the sofa. The room is crowned with a variety of valuable artwork.

Angus said of her work, "Our clients want the very best for their homes – and in this global market, good design is often copied and sold to the masses – albeit in rougher form. High-end design takes the client out of this crowd and into a rarefied world of European shopping trips, custom made furniture, and fine art."

Photography by David Duncan Livingston

PHILIP J. MEYER LTD.

Inspired by a variety of European furniture and art he planned to use in addition to the classical architectural details of his home, Philip Meyer aspired to create a worldly, but casual living space. "There were certain things the architecture wanted; it dictated formality, yet I tried to keep it less formal."

Meyer painted the walls a deep sage and the molding a bisque color to create a neutral, uniform backdrop for the pieces he wanted to display. The furniture had an air of formality, such as an eighteenth century English secretary, a nineteenth century French coaching table, and a vintage Spanish chandelier. According to Meyer, most of the art demanded formal, gilt wood frames, in keeping with the architecture, so he integrated his more traditional pieces. On the more casual side, most of the fabrics Meyer chose were either cottons, linens, or other natural fibers. The sofa was a custom down filled "tuxedo" sofa he covered in Corragio cashmere and accented with Clarence House pattern pillows, the teak dining chairs he covered in a Henry Calvin linen. "I chose each piece based on the importance of furniture, and then played down the formality with the fabrics."

Meyer's design was high-end because each piece was carefully selected and accumulated over many years of traveling the world and buying beautiful things. "I chose to live in that house with less, rather than a poor substitute. I was very particular."

Photography by David Duncan Livingston

CONSTANTIN GORGES INC.

Constantin Gorges was inspired by the client's fantastic art collection, specifically a Magritte bowler hat painting, to create a conceptual approach of viewing important art in a home that made sense, and in fact made the painting stronger. He viewed the space as an orchestra, and the painting as the first violin.

Gorges abandoned what he called "an old school approach," designing a room around an area rug, and instead he designed the space around the art. He chose to cover the upholstered pieces in blue fabric to pick up on the blue in the painting, and he added a subtle glazed stripe to reflect the sky. He designed mahogany cabinetry to provide a rich background for the painting. He could not add more art to the room because "that painting is a tough act to follow," so instead he designed a simple gold mirror to reflect the painting on the opposite wall. The other pieces he added to the room were carefully chosen based on their relation to the painting. For example, the selection of neoclassical antiques of the early nineteenth century expressed a design consistency with the art deco spirit of the 1930s, the time Magritte's bowler hat paintings represented. Gorges believed his substantial level of classical training in design and decorative arts, while not required, is what enabled him to create high-end spaces. "If a client has ten million dollar paintings, it might make sense if you know a little about it."

Gorges' design is high-end because of the level of quality of everything in the room, including the mahogany cabinetry, the rugs, fabrics, Fortuny pillows, antiques, and quality. Different designers may have different budgets and styles, but the distinguishing factor is whether the pieces they use are of high quality. He offered an example of a craftsman who may make a tacky polyester wall unit, but it is high-end because it is very well made. Gorges claimed his personal success is due to the fact that he offers both high quality and style.

Photography by Lydia Gould-Bessler

"There is a switch between interior design that exists on a customer service level, where designers help clients furnish a room, and the rare instance where a client is a philanthropist, and allows a designer to be creative." **Charles de Lisle**

TWO:
FURNITURE & FABRIC

CLODAGH

Clodagh explained her inspiration for her design: "I am a compendium of all my travels. I work with all the senses and all the elements. I have a vast interior video, thought, and poetry to draw on when working with people, so images pop up in my mind that illustrate what I think the client is all about." For this celebrity client, Clodagh was inspired to create a space where "he could entertain over forty people, but the space would not feel empty when he wanted to be alone."

In order to create a space that could be used equally for entertaining as it could a personal refuge, Clodagh focused on making the individual pieces substantial. The dining chairs were carved by hand, which gave them "tremendous energy." The Mesa dining table is strong enough "you could get six people dancing on it and it wouldn't move." Clodagh made deep window seats where the client could hang out on the phone and watch the world or have extra seating for a party. Similarly, she extended the front of the fireplace to provide a concrete bench, able to seat many people but also would pass as an architectural detail when he was home alone. To ensure the client felt like his apartment was his personal refuge, Clodagh applied a soothing plaster to the walls and ceiling, creating "an envelope," so "you feel very grounded in the apartment."

"I believe in easy living. I don't believe in creating spaces where people have to have huge maintenance problems; I want to create spaces where the pieces maintain the people."

Clodagh's approach to high-end design was to completely customize an environment for the client. "To create luxury, we have a lot of applied art studios that we work with. What gives a feeling of luxury is to have things that are clearly not off the shelf, that are purpose-built, that are custom made." Not only did Clodagh design many of the pieces in this space herself, but she also tamed natural elements to suit the design. "We work with hard materials, and give them subtle, sensual finishes that make them very stroke-able. I think you should be able to stroke your apartment and feel comfortable."

Photography by Daniel Aubry

EDWARD LOBRANO INTERIOR DESIGN INC.

Edward Lobrano wanted his bedroom "to be classic, but with a little bit of style." Inspired by his beautiful, carved bed by Gregorius/Pineo, Lobrano professed, "I want it to be handsome, tailored, and traditional. This is about me. I don't like fluffy stuff."

Lobrano built upon these ideas to create a masculine bedroom with clean lines. The linens were made with fabrics by Rose Tarlow, the elegant English Sloane side tables had leather tops, the drapery was simple and just enough to tie the windows to the rest of the fabrics. The Italian marble medallions he had bought in Paris evoked a bit of classicism in the space. "I love this apartment, it feels like home – I love being there. It is soft, handsome, pretty, and comfortable. I like a lot of modern design but if you have to live in it – it is not comfortable."

Lobrano's bedroom is high-end design because of the craftsmanship in every item in the space. "The difference between high-end and mediocre work is the quality of how things are made. You can see it on the detail of my drapery. It is all interlined, has a little cord welt, it is quality..." He added, "High-end design is good taste, it is in detail, it is quality, it is custom. You can change the size, shape, width. That is the biggest difference."

Photography by Eric Piasecki

SKB ARCHITECTURE AND DESIGN

Nestor Santa-Cruz's inspiration came from his client's desire to transform their traditional, classical shell of a Washington, D.C. townhouse into a more contemporary, fresh space. He wanted to create "a sense of tradition rendered with a soft, modern vocabulary."

Santa-Cruz sought aspects of the house he could update and streamline. He painted all the trim white, and introduced contrast with café au lait walls next to nearly-black floors. Instead of traditional drapery he incorporated a privacy screen to be "less fussy." The B&B Italia desk, with its strong lines and mix of metal and oak, set a contemporary tone for the room, but it's placement in the window with two lamps referenced traditional floor plans. The desk, when contrasted with the dark, Barbara Barry slab coffee table, added an architectural element, of "dark and light, heavy and floating," suggesting a variety of influences in the design. The two upholstered chairs have "a 1950s, Albert Hadley, Park Avenue look to them," but Santa-Cruz added a modern twist – he stylized them with a skirt.

Santa-Cruz's design is high-end because he successfully addressed the clients' needs in an aesthetically pleasing way. "It is not about how much people invest, it is not about having designer pieces or products. High-end design is founded upon having a client with an inspiration, the space or site, and a designer searching for that level of design that is not about what is in the room, but is about the client's needs or personality."

Photography by Gordon Beall

"Style is about your own personal sense of what you express in your life."

2MICHAELS DESIGN

Jayne Michaels, one-half of 2Michaels Design, wanted to create a spacious, uncluttered, serene space; one that would naturally integrate art. She also had a fantasy to live among the work of rational Italian designers from the twentieth century, and bring their work into the twenty-first century.

Starting with a large Sam Samore black and white photograph, a gift from a friend, she added an Edward Wormley sofa in a mustard-colored fabric, "a timeless hue bold enough to compliment the photograph." Michaels found a Gio Ponti wing chair, and kept it in its original fabric. A friend gave her a blue Federico Vegas oil painting, which she then worked into the room by finding pillows in mustard, blue, and olive green to add some warmth. Michaels realized she was using colors akin to Gerricho, an artist from the thirties, who tended to use muted but strong colors. The result, as Joan Michaels, the other half of 2Michaels design put it, is a space that is well-balanced: "it is both modern and antique, soft and bold, feminine and masculine."

Jayne believes this room is high-end because "each piece is a unique twentieth century antique; nothing is from a showroom or catalog, and it was done with a collector's eye and love." Joan Michaels adds that, "All the pieces are very special, and only increase in value over time."

Photography by Frank Veteran

"The pieces were chosen with an eye that had a lot of knowledge of furniture."

YOUR SPACE INTERIORS

Charles De Lisle decided that he wanted to create a "moody, sexy dining room," in this grand manor house in San Francisco's foggy, tree-lined Presidio district. His inspiration came from a few sources, including a slate blue color, an ink-brushed Japanese drawing of fog settling into the trees, and an image of a bronze Buddhist temple.

De Lisle brought the outside in by placing fifty-year-old, well-groomed giant trees in each corner and skirting them in a brick-like print. The dining table had a rich, lacquer feel to it, and above it he hung a brass centerpiece he designed: laser-cut from a photocopied detail of a Buddhist temple banner. The dining chairs, nineteenth century Swedish rococo with gilded leather seats provided a radical shift from the 1970s white table, enabling this room to be more about mood and color than any one period. De Lisle broke up the monochromatic color of the room by introducing a multicolored antique rug and pieces of texture, like the massive rope used for the drapery tiebacks. He carefully selected the art and accessories. "I wanted to make it feel like someone might have owned that room, and the art wasn't there just because it matched."

De Lisle's approach was to create "an emotional response" and "spaces with life in them that feels like an event or experience – you walk away and you remember it." His design is high-end because of the provenance of the items he selected. For example, commenting on the dining chairs, he said, "Someone who is going to buy those chairs is someone who understands what they are."

Photography by Cesar Rubio

MAUREEN WILSON FOOTER & ASSOCIATES

Maureen Footer wanted to create her own fantasy room. Her idea for this room came from a new fabric of embroidered linen from her friend, Lisa Fine. The fabric had an embroidered mirror Buddhist motif inspired by a visit to India. "The fabric had so much character, as soon as I saw it, it dictated to me the room we should do." Footer found the fabric to be whimsical and exotic, but at the same time fresh and Western. The fabric suggested "Oriental luxury," "repose," and a "mogul tent," which became the idea behind the structure of the room.

"I like rooms that are very classical, but have an unexpected interpretation." Fittingly, she took this intimate, square room and transformed it into a mesmerizing, canopied boudoir for a worldly, sophisticated maharani. Footer carried the silvery, mirror motif of the fabric in many places, including an Art Deco French mirror with a detailing on top that resembled a bejeweled turban, a Venetian mirror, a silver finish on the mantel and base boards, the chandelier, and the sequined-ball trim on the drapery. She wanted to convey material richness and ease, so she added luxurious touches such as a curly, silky, soft, lamb fur rug, a cashmere throw, and velvet covered stools. A lamp by John Copper integrated a pomegranate motif, which is the Indian mogul motif for hospitality. Using a rich spectrum of luxurious textures, light sources, and things to look at was in keeping with Footer's design aesthetic. "My approach has always been to produce work that is sensual, rooms that people want to walk barefoot in, sit down and read a book in, that respond to sensory perceptions as well as visual ones."

Footer stated, it is "the quality of the goods, conception, and execution which makes it a room that stands alone in terms of quality."

Photography by Laurie Lambrecht

WHEELER DESIGN GROUP

Marion Wheeler was inspired by the color of the ocean. This house had fantastic views of the Pacific and she wanted to carry the color into the master bedroom. She settled on a palette of blue tones with bits of dark contrast for visual interest. "I am a drama person, I like a lot of contrast," she explained.

Wheeler liked to juxtapose the traditional with the modern, and monochromatic blues with high contrast black and copper. Starting with a greyed-down sea blue drapery, Wheeler matched the wall color. The bedspread is the same blue color in a sheer fabric, but has a copper lining underneath for added richness. Wheeler mixed the furniture, such as a contemporary, stylized wingchair and a vintage art deco bench. She installed a large antique black Chinoiserie secretary for drama, power, and punch, and to balance the headboard on the other side of the room.

Wheeler's design is high-end because of her successful selection of contrasting pieces. As she said, "It's not crisp, but it is powerful."

Photography by David Duncan Livingston

WICK DESIGN GROUP

Will Wick summed up the challenge of this project as, "How to keep this a formal-looking living room but make it user friendly." Inspired by the client's desire to give their living room a "younger look," Wick turned to furniture pieces and a color palette that had a "hip, playful edge."

"My preferred aesthetic is beach-like; bleached woods with a soft, natural, organic look." He started by adding a Persian rug, and then set about creating a light, natural environment. A comfortable sofa and tufted club chairs gave the room a young, funky look. The floor lamp added a unique sculptural element. Instead of adding a large, solid coffee table, and in keeping with the vein of the natural wood going throughout the room, Wick incorporated a glass table and two acacia wood stools. Wick added, "since we wanted to make this a friendly, usable environment, instead of having a 60-inch plasma on the wall, we encased it in the cabinet," which he designed. The final modern touch was a few pieces of art, including pieces by Nathan Olivera and Geoffrey Key.

"'High-end' is defined by an unwavering commitment to quality in every aspect of the design of a project. It is about not compromising appropriate design to get it done cheaper, or more quickly. This being said, I don't necessarily equate a large price tag with 'high-end' design. I find quality in form, and that doesn't always mean 'expensive'. Some of my best pieces come from 'deals' I get at the flea markets. They so nicely enrich the provenance of a home. They have history."

Photography by David Duncan Livingston

WILLIAM MCINTOSH DESIGN

McIntosh combined his modernist aesthetic with his clients' more traditional interests. The client had an interest in acquiring Beidermaier and traditional English furniture, so McIntosh balanced the look with "a strong, modern background," so one could "read the profiles more distinctively." He explained, "It is a modern apartment in a modern building, packed with the latest technology and mechanical systems, but it is not steel and chrome modernism. It is a little plusher, more comfortable, and references traditional and historical things."

McIntosh started with the floor plan. "My work is about spatial arrangements, getting the backgrounds right, redefining the architecture." The room, a giant east-west expanse, was to be an all-in-one living room, home office, and "loungey" reading area. McIntosh defined the edge of the living area by building a cabinet/display case and backing the sofa up to it. He selected some George Smith upholstery and designed a sycamore coffee table that resembled 1940s French furniture. He paneled the walls and hung paintings on hanging rods – an effect that referenced a more traditional style. The color palette was also a mix, including butter yellow, and mossy green, colors that are "not colorful, not bright." McIntosh added, "I like colors that are unclear as to what they are."

McIntosh's design is high-end because of the immense care and expense applied to every aspect of the project, even the simple, contemporary lines of the architecture. "To get things that simple takes an awful lot of work." He added, "quality will cost you, there is no cheap way out."

Photography by Billy Cunningham

ANN GETTY & ASSOCIATES

Ann Getty aspired to create a nineteenth century gentleman's library, complete with botany, geography, astronomy, and some great English literature. The room was to be cozy but formal at the same time, true to what would have been in such a library.

Getty started with the floor plan. She divided the large, square room into a sitting area and a writing area. Many of the pieces in the room are from Getty's line of high-end reproduction furniture. The colors are muted, but many-colored, including pale green, coral, and beige. When layered together in the room, the colors balance, leaving a cheery, multi-faceted space to look at. To display the groups of objects, Getty clustered them together for impact. "I don't like clutter, I like cluster." She clustered globes, maps, mushroom and floral botanical models.

"The room is high-end because it has antiques and reproductions of beautiful pieces with beautiful lines; it is a very comfortable room." Getty believed the quality and craftsmanship of the details made this room high-end. "High-end is quite flawless, I hope."

Photography by Phillip Ennis

"There is a lot of great design that is modern, easier to afford, but it is not high-end. The price reflects a level of craftsmanship."

TWO:
FURNITURE & FABRIC

DAVID DESMOND, INC.

David Desmond was inspired to create a high energy, bright, happy room. He chose red and gold; a "strong, good luck, happy" set of colors as his palette, integrating in a bit of blue to cover the full color spectrum. "I often find that rooms with those three colors feel good," he explained.

Starting with squares of Dutch metal leaf over a dark brown lacquer, Desmond layered on more color with the bright rug and the Colefax & Fowler multicolor drapery fabric. He added green silk throw pillows and linen check fabric on the daybed. Desmond added a number of elements to tone down his strong color palette, such as the sisal rug underneath the woven rug. The white chairs provide a needed reprieve from the intense color, keeping the room in balance.

Desmond's project is high-end because of the custom finishes, such as the walls, and the immense level of detail, such as the drapery construction. He said of high-end, "It should be satisfying on an immediate level, but also as you spend time in the room you can enjoy it more because someone has obviously thought of things that make it comfortable for you and delightful for you as a visual aesthetic experience."

Photography by Douglas Hill

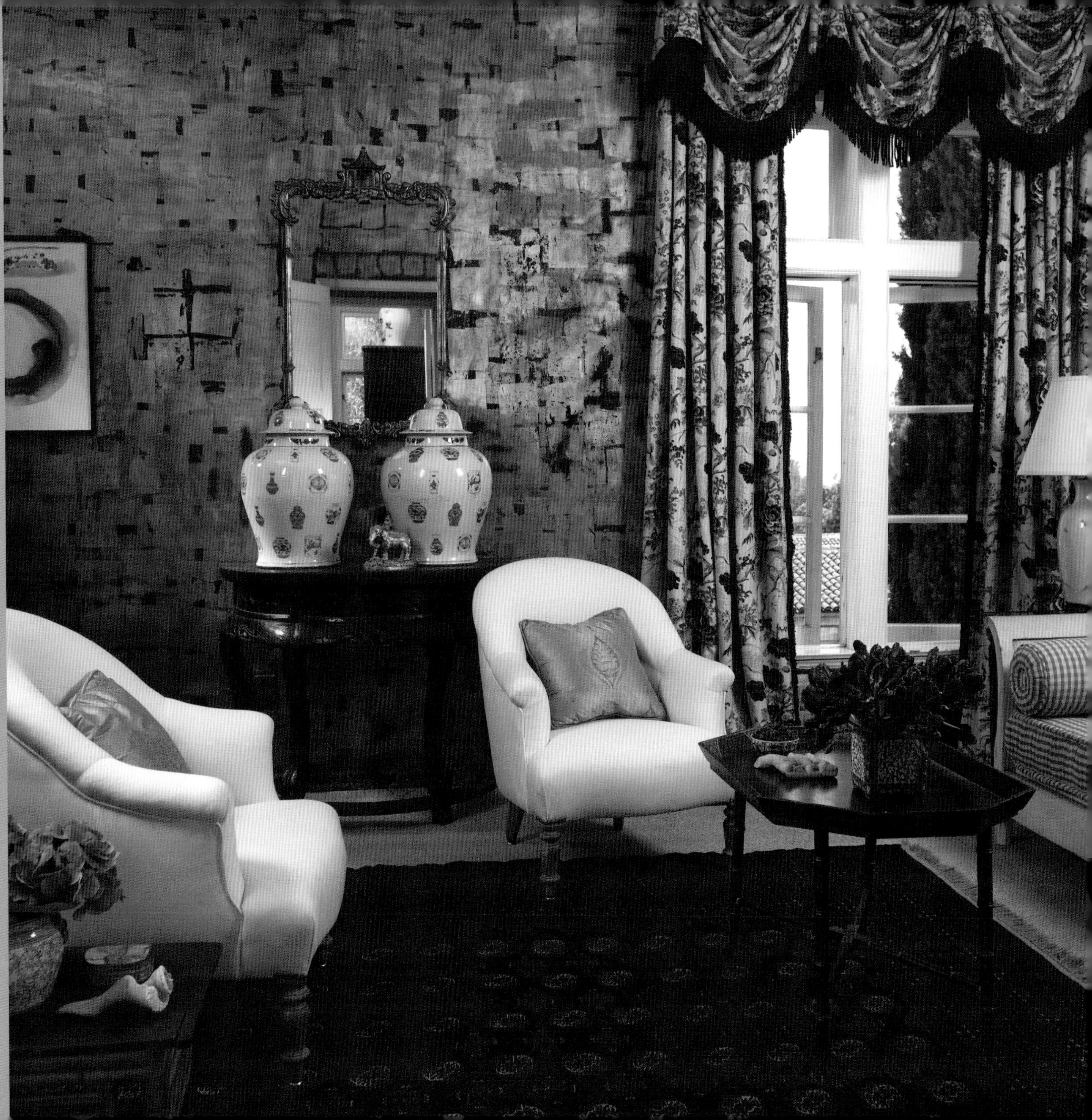

ASHLEY ROI JENKINS DESIGN

Ashley Jenkins was inspired to make this powder room "moody, sexy, glamorous, and dark." She had Maya Romanoff custom color beaded wallpaper a chocolate brown, and that element set the rhythm of her design.

Jenkins extended her deep color palette to the drapery fabric – a contemporary horizontal stripe in saturated colors. The mirror, an ornate piece with warm, copper-colored glass, housed a small television screen. The sink, copper and nickel in color, was mounted on a reproduction of an intricate seventeenth century Russian writing desk. She chose the chocolate marble floor to sweep the eye through the space and the sparkling Boyd light fixtures to stop them.

Jenkins' design is high-end because it is well-trained and creative at the same time. She claimed, "A high-end designer is someone who has a grasp of history, furniture, and art, and what is happening currently in the design industry, and can put that together in a way that functions well."

Photography by David Duncan Livingston

MATTHEWS STUDIO

Nestor Matthews challenged himself to design a Bay Area bedroom in the cool colors of the fog, but one that would still be inviting for a woman. Focusing on the color and texture of fog, he created a tranquil, sweet retreat.

Matthews started by applying a blue glaze over grey walls, "to bring the sky in the room." He then added a little deeper blue-grey luxurious linen for the drapery. The wool carpet offered a soft wheat background, and he covered the bed in three different rich materials. Matthews found mixing textures not only evoked the fog well, but also made the space tactile, and more interesting to the viewer. In order to keep the space from being "dull," Matthews added bits of orange and red to contrast the cool tones.

Matthews work is high-end because he pushed a few ideas. His unabashed use of blues solidified a mood and his choice of art increased the scale of the room. He said, "there is a certain boldness of design moves you need to take to make it a creative room." He added, "High-end is design where people are willing to take a few more risks, and try some new ideas."

Photography by Ken Gutmaker

KENNETH HOCKIN INTERIORS

To create this living room, Kenneth Hockin was charged with merging two previous household styles – hers was formal, his was casual. "We were trying to make the whole room feel much more casual," he claimed. "We were looking for texture and for something that is fun. I think a lot of people forget about having fun in a room."

Hockin looked to add elements that would loosen up some of the more formal pieces of furniture in the room, while bringing unity to the design. "We wanted to make the chair like a piece of art," he explained, so he covered it in striking black and white Donghia fabric. "I love adding elements of black to any room. If you have a room that is all over the place in terms of colors and textures, touches of black round out the room and it is very subtle." Similarly, the casual, circular, hat straw rug "worked because it brought these high styled pieces of furniture down a notch."

Hockin's design is high-end because, "while there is a big mix in this room, the level of quality of everything is at the highest." To Hockin, "high-end design means there is a mutual understanding that while we may have particular ideas about what a particular piece of furniture might be, we are seeking something of the highest quality." He added, "You really can't do a satisfying traditional room without selecting pieces of high quality. It is the detailing of the furniture that reveals the quality. If someone is working on a limited budget, I often encourage them to do something simpler, more contemporary."

Photography by Nancy Elizabeth Hill

ANGELA FREE INTERIOR DESIGN

Angela Free was inspired by a collection of fabrics to create a pretty, feminine master bedroom that would also appeal to men. "It's very important to be gender-sensitive in a room. Particularly in a bedroom," she explained.

Free pulled together a color palette of softer, slightly feminine colored fabrics in a variety of textures. "It's a textural story, not a print story," she explained, adding that there were very few patterns in the room. The feminine touch came across by the mix of curvilinear pieces, the whimsical floating of the furniture in the middle of the room, and the architectural details she added such as the curved window lambrequin and the crosshatched, linen-like painted wall finish.

Free's design is high-end because she built her design through subtle layering of textures rather than relying on loud prints or patterns. Such precise understanding of how different sheens of the same color white paint or different materials of the same color fabric takes experience and skill.

Photography by Matthew Millman

"High-end design is the ability to acquire the best objects that you can afford and that you can lay your hands on. Anybody can design a sofa or put wallpaper on the walls, but to know how to collect these jewelry pieces, … that is high-end design – using materials that are old and new, rich and poor, doing that in a way that is luscious, luxury oriented. High-end, for me, is finding the right piece for a room that shows that you have high-end taste. High-end is the ability to spend the right kind of money on the right thing or things. It is the way you shop."
– Mark Zeff

THREE:
PERSONALITY or
CONCEPT

TUCKER & MARKS, INC.

Suzanne Tucker was inspired by this San Francisco building's French heritage, and thus had Paris on her mind when she set out to design these rooms. "I have always loved Coco Chanel's apartment on the Rue Cambon – elegant, very rich, fabulous…"

Tucker said of Chez Chanel, "it had a tawny palette of ambers, blacks, and golds that my client and I loved. So I chose a palette of rich neutral tones – chocolates, buttery beiges, and honey golds." Tucker painted the dining room walls a dark lacquered brown and haloed the dome ceiling in gold. The dark walls needed contrasting decoration, so she hung a pair of antique ornate gilt mirrors over Italian Baroque console twins from Christies. The chandelier, a decorative Louis XV-style gilt piece lit by two-dozen candles, gave the room a romantic glow and ethereal feel. It was simply, "magnificently magical."

Tucker decided to play up the building's curved corners and façade of curved bay windows on the interior. The entrance hall, once square, became round, and instead of using traditional diamond-shape cabochons in the slab marble floor, she used dark brown circles. Continuing the circular theme, she designed a high-gloss, radial-herringbone-patterned wood floor inlaid with ebony and added a beautiful antique round dining table.

Tucker's work in this apartment is nothing short of high-end. The rich colors, valuable pieces, and thoughtful creativity she employed to design the space in the spirit of Coco Chanel exude luxury.

Photography by Tim Street-Porter

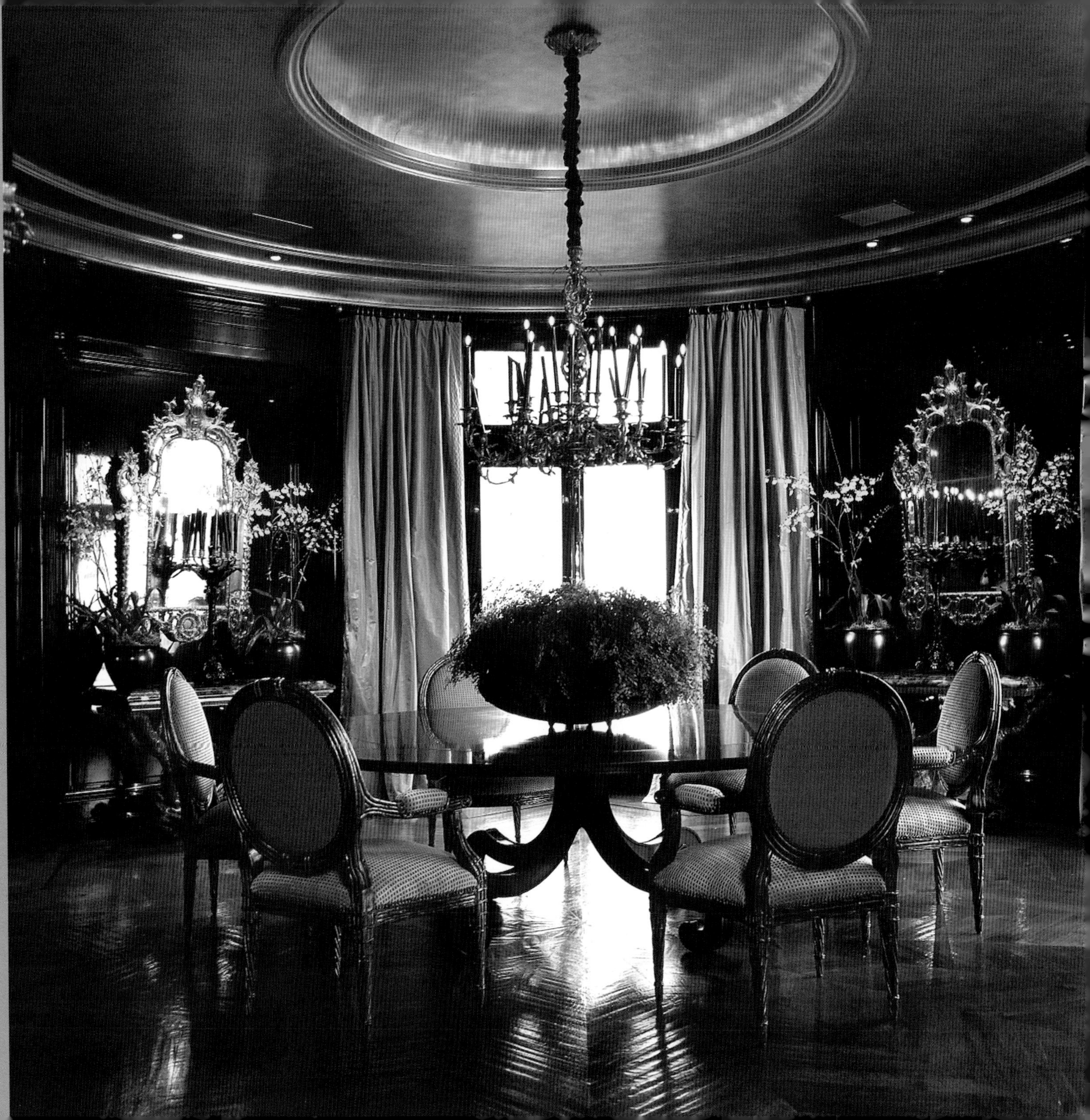

THE JEFFREY DESIGN GROUP

Noel Jeffrey was inspired to take this grand scale, formal dining room and make it more intimate and inviting. He also wanted to integrate the garden on the outside with the aesthetic on the inside, "to create the feeling of a garden indoors." The result was a comfortable, whimsical dining room fit for large groups or an intimate dinner for two.

Key to Jeffrey's design was to abandon a traditional dining room structure, a single table below a chandelier centered in the middle of the room. Instead, he incorporated a large round table and a smaller table by the fireplace. Jeffrey's room layout encouraged relaxation, as did the less formal, friendly, checkered drapery. Within this less formal environment, Jeffrey was able to integrate fabulous antiques without being too stuffy. The dining chairs were nineteenth century English, the buffet was late nineteenth century French, and the mirror was a spectacular Chippendale piece that added just the needed amount of whimsy to the room. Rather than opting for a serious area rug, Jeffrey stained the floors a light gold-checkered pattern.

Jeffrey's design is high-end because of the quality of documented antiques and art he integrated into the room. Every piece was valuable; there were no reproductions. Jeffrey stated that high-end design "includes very high quality, it includes attention to detail, it includes a knowledge on the designers part of the pieces of period furniture one would use, and it requires an extremely refined understanding of interior architecture."

Photography by Mick Hales

JONES FOOTER MARGEOTES PARTNERS ARCHITECTURE & INTERIOR DESIGN

Kerry Delrose wanted to create a kitchen fit for a glamorous dinner party. "Kitchens are the most overlooked rooms in the whole house," he said. They tend to "not be very visual," and "rarely are a place to hang art." Delrose wanted to create a kitchen that doubled as an entertaining space, large enough to fit seven or eight people. "I wanted it to be young and sexy, you never hear that about a kitchen."

Delrose added a bit of elegance to every aspect of the kitchen. To dress up the space he added modern art and photographs matted in chocolate suede. He designed the unique klismos-like chairs and added heavy mahogany on the back and mohair on the seat. He added an eye-catching, octagonal dining table and top quality linen wallpaper in the window area. A chrome and distressed leather chair by Ralph Lauren and nickel-plated fixtures from Waterworks added more glam. The Duplo Dynamico fan, which moves up and down while spinning, gave the space a wild, architectural element "to make the space fun, not just a place you come in to turn on the stove." He added, "I wanted you to be able to throw a dinner party in there."

Delrose's design was high-end because the products were "the best of the best." The rich fabrics, furniture, and accessories did not have pattern or a high degree of ornamentation, but Delrose chose them for this luxurious kitchen because upon close inspection their quality would speak for itself. He advised, "there are certain things that are so great, so elegant, people should make the investment," if given the resources, and called it "investment decorating."

Photography by Phillip Ennis

HAYSLIP DESIGN ASSOCIATES

Sherry Hayslip aspired to "bring fresh eyes to Cape Cod style." While she chose to adhere to many aspects of traditional New England design for this beach house, she offered a new perspective – "simple and natural."

In keeping with New England style, Hayslip retained the oversized, intricate moldings, but painted them white and covered the walls in a hand-troweled raw plaster of a creamy, fleshy color. She wanted to "add warmth but still be neutral to set off the color of water and the beach." The effect was a simple, elegant negative space relief for the furniture. Hayslip selected fabrics in natural fibers – no synthetics allowed – in light, neutral colors. With all the bright Cape sunlight, "the space glows with a sense of serenity and calmness."

Hayslip offers that it is the rarity and uniqueness of the objects that makes a room high-end. "There is a distinct level of connoisseurship that extends to every object." In this space, the exquisite quality of objects and artifacts that Hayslip selected include the client's world-class sea shell collection, a found tortoise shell on the mantle, and hand-carved wooden shells on the back of the dining chairs. Even the floors were hand scraped and rubbed with pigment to almost look like sand.

Photography by John Smith

JEFFERS DESIGN GROUP

Jay Jeffers wanted to create a space that represented his client – a young, female, San Francisco spa owner, someone who "loves glamour but also loves jeans." Looking to create a space that felt "feminine, fluffy, and fun," Jeffers incorporated plush fabrics and a powdery color palette.

The windows were a key element to Jeffers' design, which he played up by coloring them as opposed to the surrounding wall. The Donghia daybed was the perfect fit for the style of the space, and the vintage armchair gave soul to the place. He added touches of blues, greens, sparkle, and tufting to give the room "a dressy feel." The coffee table by John Charles Joan contributed to the light, airy feeling.

Jeffers' design is high-end because of his focus on quality and his ability to find and work with fantastic pieces. "I always look for the best quality pieces, if they are old they have to be maintained well." Jay has an eye for special pieces. "I don't like recognizable pieces. I would rather walk into a room, love the room, and not recognize things."

Photography by Cesar Rubio

SCOTT SANDERS L.L.C.

Scott Sanders aspired to create "The Great American TV Room." Unlike so many basement media rooms, which are cold, dark, and rarely used, Sanders wanted this room to be an often-used, fabulous television game room. Sanders' design inspiration came from some multi-colored Saccho runners which he had sewn together to make a full rug. He was drawn to the colors, which carried a 1970s color palette of avocado green, chocolate brown, cherry red, and yellow – perfect to create a "vintage '70s family room with a modern twist."

From there, Sanders added comfortable, chocolate brown leather sofas. He painted the walls a happy yellow so that "you wouldn't know you were in the basement." Using what he calls "the high-low method," he mixed a variety of furniture, fit for a kid-friendly, high-end family room. The pieces included Ralph Lauren club chairs, and Holly Hunt coffee tables, mixed with Crate & Barrel Windsor chairs he transformed by lacquering them. For accessories, he transformed vintage TV Guides, TV-themed lunch boxes, and blueprints from popular sitcom houses into artwork by displaying them in frames and shadow boxes.

Sanders' design is high-end because "everything is pulled to-gether." He added so many elegant and unexpected details for a basement room, such as full drapery, sconces, throw pillows, wall-to-wall sea grass under the area rugs, and more. That the depth of the design is very apparent. "I went all the way," he said.

Photography by Pat Miller

TODD KLEIN, INC.

Todd Klein was inspired by a photograph of a bathroom in Dorset belonging to T.E. Lawrence (Lawrence of Arabia). The grand bathroom, filled with meaningful memoirs and travel souvenirs, was designed to be the "true home" of the house.

Klein designed his "bathroom with a worldly view" with luxuries such as a copper and zinc soaking tub, a fireplace, and valuable accessories. The mantel, with an intricately designed, eglomise reverse painted glass Chinoiserie patterned piece, displayed personal snapshots to evoke a sense of intimacy. Above the Japanese altar he hung a large Japanese screen made of a collage of ancient Japanese textiles with a luxurious silver leaf background. The floor, a linoleum, also looked like silver leaf. "This is a place I would want to go to feel safe and nurtured, cocooned, a room of my own." The room's worldly references inspired dreaming, meditation, and fantasy. This was perfect for Klein, who said, "You always want to be where you are not."

Klein's design is high-end because "It is custom fitted for some person's vision for what they wanted, like a custom fitted suit." He added, that although the mantle, tub, and screen are fabulously valuable pieces, "Items don't have to be expensive, but the room needs to come together in a way that is high-end. To me, it's about being personalized and detailed."

Photography by Kelly Bugden

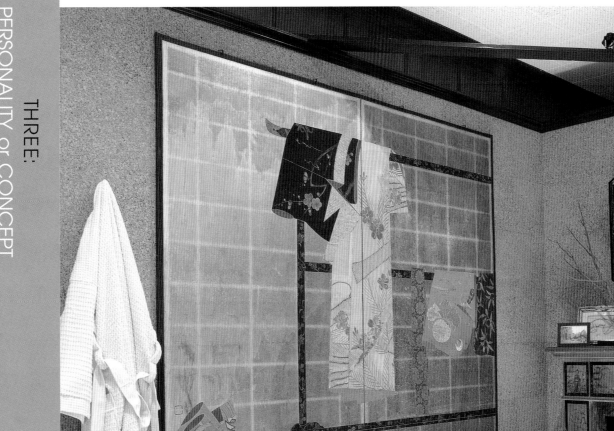

JEAN ALAN

Jean Alan wanted to create a living/entertaining area that accurately represented her client's young, ambitious, unconventional personality. "He wanted a mid-century kind of feel but did not want to go with any of the mid-century kinds of conventions." Rather, "everything was more European or more eccentric," and chosen for its fit with his art collection.

In keeping with the plan to create a unique space, Alan custom-made a curved sofa and upholstered it in mohair. She selected a 1950s, handmade French oak coffee table and a Plexiglass chair upholstered in sheepskin. An Italian mahogany console, a Lucite and brass lamp attributed to Carl Springer, and a 1960s Scandinavian leather chair added to the collection. While Alan did introduce exquisite objects into the space, she purposefully did not let any one object scream for attention, and reduced some background contrast to better offset the artwork. She added rich, heavyweight linen drapes, window shades the same color as the walls, and introduced an Odegard rug because of it "mellow" shades of green. In the adjoining room, Alan had Herman Miller build custom cabinets to match the wall paint. "Everything fits. There is no one gorgeous object, the space has a real sense of balance; it is coherent."

Alan's work is high-end due to "the uniqueness of every object you see and the coherence of the outcome."

Photography by Michael Robinson

KATHRYN SCOTT DESIGN STUDIO LTD.

Kathryn Scott wanted to design a home that would properly blend her American roots with that of her Chinese installation artist husband, Wenda Gu. She was "trying to combine both cultures in a way that felt comfortable."

Scott chose specific pieces to reflect her exposure to Chinese culture and her American heritage. The custom Chinese cocktail table has a unique, white marble top carved out of one piece of stone. Scott designed the red chairs with a "bit of a [Western] woman's skirt" on them. The cabinet was based on an Asian design, and manufactured in China. The antique rug, secretary, and small table were passed down through her family, while the many valuable Chinese artifacts and sculptures represent Gu's cultural background. Scott described her design as a "series of discoveries – you may not see everything at first glance." The result is "there are little signs of both of us throughout," creating an intimate, personalized space.

She believes, "good design is not about creating a space that looks like a showroom; it is about creating a picture of who you are and what is sentimental to you." She added, "I wouldn't want to walk into someone's home and not know who lives there."

Photography by Tom Sibley

RUBY, INC.

Inspired by her client's personality and love for high-class entertaining, Bella Zakarian created an elegant, formal entertaining salon with a female sensibility. The apartment came with a heightened sense of style, as Edward Wormley had designed all the built-ins with the previous owner. Zakarian went for simple elegance in an old Hollywood glamour kind of way, so "you want to have a glass of champagne in there."

In one of the two seating areas, Zakarian covered the scroll back chairs in a deep purple. The French antique coffee table, from 145 Antiques, is delicate and beautiful, with a blue mirror top, in a charming, "not too pristine," condition. The lamp is Murano glass from the 1950s. Zakarian wanted to keep the drapery simple and elegant, so she layered a pale blue taffeta over a white sheer from Rogers and Goffigon. When the drapery blocked the client's view of Central Park, Zakarian, who typically never uses tiebacks, found the perfect solution – white feather boas. The boas fit the feminine, elegant nature of the room, so that "you felt you might wear the room; it might become a dress."

Zakarian's room is high-end because "every piece is special and thoughtfully put together." The client cared about collecting, so visitors "want to examine every piece." Zakarian added, "I don't think it has to have a high price tag to make it high-end, it is about putting thought in the space."

Photography by Johnny Miller

"I make people think about things they have not thought about before."

KATHRYN WALTZER
INTERIOR DESIGN

Kathryn Waltzer claims she tries to incorporate her client's personality in each of her projects. This client, a frequent enter-tainer, was sophisticated, and also exuded machismo. Fittingly, Walzter began her design with the "masculine, entertaining colors" of cognac.

Picking up on the colors seen in the decanters at the client's bar – cognac, gold, and brown – Waltzer then sprinkled them across the room and complimented them with soft, pale blue. Going for a simple, spare 1940s Hollywood luxury look, Walzter "wanted a visually stunning, but soothing space." Plush sofas, floating out from the wall, an antique Chinese cabinet, and an antique French wrought iron chair gave shape to the room. She separated the large space with two rugs and two seating groups, "so it didn't feel like a hotel lobby," and used luscious-to-touch materials such as silk, chenille, and velvet.

Waltzer's design is high-end because "the mindset is high-end." She added, "It's very sophisticated, from the budget to the fabrics; it's a high-end way of living. Not everyone wants to live with silk chairs or Oriental rugs." She concluded, "This place is an experience. It's a mood – that's what is high-end about it."

Photography by Dominique Vorillon

GRANT K. GIBSON
INTERIOR DESIGN

Grant Gibson wanted to create "a feminine room, an elegant room; a place a woman can feel beautiful in." Gibson wanted his design to be "simple, like the little black dress itself." He incorporated references to Audrey Hepburn and *Breakfast at Tiffany's* to evoke a notion of classic beauty.

Gibson went so far as to celebrate the little black dress by incorporating black couture dresses throughout history into the design of the room. He contrasted the dresses with a white high-gloss floor, creating a fantasy, make-believe dream world where "a woman might twirl as if floating around the space in front of the floor length mirror." Gibson wanted to be graphic and modern, so he included only black and white objects, in many shades to allow for striking contrast with subtle layering. He designed the drapes to puddle on the floor, resembling the train of a woman's dress.

"A room like this is not something the average person would have," Gibson stated. To Gibson, "High-end is not about mass-produced items. It is taking something that is a little bit different and having fun with it, and making it your own…"

Photography by David Duncan Livingston .

DANA NICHOLSON STUDIO INC.

Dana Nicholson said of his work, "I typically shoot over the top, fantasize unrealistically, and then tone it down to reflect the client's interest." For this project, Nicholson wanted to create a "sexy, youthful" space.

Nicholson encouraged his clients to select art first, and then built an interior to best suit the art. "It should be elegant and sexy without being too fussy," he claimed. Working in neutral colors, he custom designed the sofa, added a small pair of leather chairs and an Egg chair. The sturdy, sculptural coffee table was designed by artist Michele Oka Doner. It is "art with a great amount of function and sensibility to it." Nicholson designed several of the pieces, including the tubular light fixtures, and added a custom woven floor covering to maintain the casual feel.

Dana Nicholson's design is high-end because he successfully attended to every detail of the project. "High-end projects are well built, masterly detailed, and unique, but not trendy, nor a representative of the current trends and fads."

Photography by Steven Barker

SHERRILL CANET INTERIORS, LTD.

Sherrill Canet wanted to create a blend of old world feeling with a clean look for her client's formal entertaining area. Starting with antique Chinoiserie cabinets, Canet created a tailored look using neutral colors and various other Asian-influenced touches.

Canet created a serene living/dining space by layering neutral tones of sisal, woods, and natural cloths, avoiding high contrast colors and patterns. The living room is painted a soothing cocoa color, and Canet covered the sofa in rich linen, the club chairs in ivory velvet, and designed the drapery in an ivory raw silk. "This room is a study in texture," she claimed, and she chose such luxurious fabrics because "it is difficult to use anything else."

Canet's space is high-end because "everything is custom-made, which immediately throws it into high-end." Canet's said her design is "sleek, sophisticated, streamlined, and inviting, and that is hard to do. Something that feels really put together does not always feel comfortable. This room feels comfortable."

Photography by Mark Samu

KARI WHITMAN INTERIORS

Kari Whitman aspired to create a sexy, playful bathing-steaming experience for her bachelor client. While she wanted to stay with the contemporary aesthetic of the house, for the bath she chose an Asian theme "because it can be modern, but not cold."

In keeping with her theme, she installed an old Chinese medicine cabinet as a double vanity, with an elegant travertine marble slab on top. She hung handsome antique lanterns from the ceiling, and to create privacy for the tub window she installed an Asian-inspired glass with a slightly patterned paper lining. Whitman mixed the wall paint and glazes herself, as she explained, "It's like cooking – a little of this, a little of that – then you get the right color." She wanted the bath to be a place he might entertain, and justifiably designed a unique transparent glass side to the tub, perfect for people watching.

Whitman's design is high-end because she used high quality materials in new ways to complete an evocative concept. "As a designer doing a whole house, there should be a few rooms when people walk in they should say 'wow' – this is one of those rooms."

Photography by Christopher Covey

MADELINE GELIS INC.

For this Bozeman, Montana, estate, Madeline Gelis was inspired to create a Western home with a worldly perspective. "It feels Western, but upon closer inspection you see objects from various cultures." The result, she believed, was an "earthy elegance."

Gelis juxtaposed Western-inspired elements, such as a distressed leather armchair and sofas covered in fabric resembling early twentieth century Western print chenilles. She added prairie-style stained glass windows inspired by Frank Lloyd Wright and chose reclaimed floors and beams to provide a richness and historical perspective to the space. At the same time, the space was not entirely dictated by a classic plains aesthetic. Instead of Navajo blankets and moose heads, Gelis interlaced the room with objects from the clients' travels to Africa and Asia. The international elements included a Tibetan cabinet, African decorative accessories, antique prints from Egypt, and Tibetan carpets. As Gelis aptly put it, "If only the people from these cultures got along as well as their objects…"

Gelis' design is high-end because, "It takes skill and training to take objects that someone has a sentimental attachment to, take new pieces along with antiques, and have them all seamlessly work together."

Photography by Will Brewster

CODDINGTON DESIGN

Melanie Coddington "wanted people to walk in and have a sense of openness, spaciousness, and relaxation" for this guest room. "It was meant to be a relaxing retreat for a guest with touches of natural elements throughout and an emphasis on luxury."

Coddington worked with a soothing color palette with her pale walls, custom wool bed cover and contrasting flange, and custom silk drapes. The antique mirror fireplace surround, silver leaf chandelier, and hand blown Venetian glass floor lamp with gold flecks kept the space feeling light and dreamy, while the Regency style maple and ebony inlaid display cabinet grounded the room. She added a few pieces from nature, such as a bird's nest, for interest and the comforting effect of natural elements.

Coddington's design is high-end because every piece in the room was selected or designed to perfection. "The difference with high-end design is you are not cutting corners, you are doing everything right. You get the opportunity to fix everything, and start from scratch." She added, "It is about a luxuriousness of materials, a quality of design, and furniture."

Photography by Melissa Castro

ALICE WILEY ASSOCIATES LLC

Alice Wiley said, "color is my driving force," and it was color that guided her decisions for this Pebble Beach estate. "One of the most unappreciated elements in design is how colors look different in different lights," she added. Wiley went through great lengths to test all the colors for this project in the actual light.

Wiley took her color direction from the ocean. "We wanted soft hues, blues and greens, that would work with the color and the environment." For this living/dining room, she chose a gentle green wall color and worked from there. She added soft green chairs and an Aubusson rug on the floor. She added, "We wanted it to be happy, light, and friendly yet sophisticated," so she mixed booth formal and somewhat more casual elements, all within her ocean-inspired palette.

Wiley's design is high-end because every aspect of the space was planned and considered for its contribution to the overall design. "High-end takes a great deal of thought and objectivity," she stated.

Photography by David Duncan Livingston

BARBARA OSTROM ASSOCIATES

Barbara Ostrom was inspired to make a "wonderful romantic room" in classical eighteenth century colors, but designed for a "sensual woman of today." Ostrom believed that unlike other rooms in the house, such as libraries, living and dining rooms, spaces typically designed with both genders in mind, the master bedroom should be feminine. "Even men feel more comfortable in a feminine bedroom."

Building on her concept, Ostrom added all the decorative moldings and used original eighteenth century colors – two shades of green and a lavender. She commissioned the ceiling to be painted in Robert Adam's aesthetic. With fabrics from Beacon Hill and furniture from Swaim and antique dealers, Ostrom successfully designed an inviting bedroom retreat. The canopy over the bed and luxurious tufting in the drapery empha-sized the romantic nature of the room, as did the natural floral aromas that drift into the space from the garden outside.

Ostrom's design is high-end because of the combination of antiques and furniture, "You walk in the room and you know the person is of a certain taste level." Each item in the room was carefully chosen and to the proper scale. "Each piece relates off the next one – there is a rhythm."

Photography by Phillip Ennis

"High-end is design you don't have to think about anymore once it is done." **Darren Henault**

FOUR:
COLOR

DE SOUSA HUGHES

Geoffrey De Sousa wanted to create a chic, soothing, glamorous dining room that embodied the notion of the circle of friendship, life, and family.

The room was not extraordinary; on the contrary, it was nondescript and boxy. "It had no view, no great architecture, so we had to bring in all the interest," De Sousa assessed. He was eager to make the room "a little retro-feeling," when he stumbled across powder blue Flokati rugs then that set the color palette for the room. He had the rugs sewn together to form a circle and then painted five shades of light blue vertical lines on the walls to add height and character. The light fixture, made with lighting designer Robert Russell of New York to look Sputnik-like, incorporated Swarovski crystal, and provided an eye-stopping focal point for the space. The white patent leather chairs were based on a 1950s Harvey Probber design and surround an eighteenth century Irish breakfast table. The table centerpiece is an upside-down "precursor to the disco ball," from a 1940s dance hall in San Francisco.

De Sousa's room is high-end because, as said, he "took a combination of elements from different time periods and styles and used them together successfully." He adds, "Good designers have a sense to take chances."

Photography by David Duncan Livingston

DRAKE DESIGN ASSOCIATES

For this Hamptons show house, Jamie Drake wanted to evoke a feeling of "classic Southampton style in a modern idiom." He was inspired to show "how a summer house near the ocean could be sparkling and glamorous."

To achieve a glamorous look, Drake selected a four-poster bed with glass rods from his furniture collection to be the centerpiece. The bedside tables, which he designed as well, "resemble 1930s mirrored furniture made in a twenty-first century way." He covered the ceiling in a silvered, natural linen fabric in order to have "the contrast of the linen, which is a typical summer, beachy kind of fabric, and the silver, to give it glitter, shine, and luster."

The wallpaper was hand blocked, in a custom-colored pale blue that was "very modernist in its sensibility and pattern" with a woven, textured feeling. Drake designed the curtains to be ethereal, with pale blue silk taffeta, which reminded him of "the ocean as it rolls onto the beach." Other chic pieces designed by Drake included a custom chaise covered in a "Chanel-like tweedy boucle" and a stripped Louis XV Swag chair in a blue ultra-suede.

Drake believes a number of elements in his design connote high-end design. "Starting with customization – the wall covering, the custom-stained floor, the made-to-order upholstery." Other luxury elements included the materials used, such as real crystal, and the lavishness of a stained parchment desk. And finally, Drake incorporated valuable antiques. Drake attests that high-end design is "Having something that is unique and special."

Photography by Eric Striffler

THRASHER DESIGN COMPANY

The client for this project hired Jeffrey Thrasher based on his response to her request that he send her an image of an interior that he finds beautiful. Thrasher built on this initial connection and designed a space to suit his client's personality – happy, positive, upbeat, and social.

Thrasher created a space that upon entry, "your sense of sight is heightened." He employed rich, saturated colors, bold curvy pieces, and alluring art. Simultaneously, the brushed travertine floor looks centuries old and it "gives weight to the space; it grounds it." The result is colorful space that is not overdone, just cheery.

Several signature pieces by such luxury furniture designers as Wendell Castle and Christian Augustville, are mixed in with valuable vintage pieces such as the sofa. "I like to find beautiful things that have beautiful finishes and a bit of history to them… It reads very clearly, this is a high-end project."

Photography by Eric Laignel

CHRISTOPHER COLEMAN
INTERIOR DESIGN

Chris Coleman's inspiration for this room came from the rest of the apartment, which was strongly influenced by the client's taste for color, pattern, and excitement. Coleman wanted the dining room to be a natural extension of the rest of his design, but also the quietest room in the house.

Coleman integrated requests from the client, such as the use of bright, tropical colors, and the replacement of traditional wood with contemporary metal, glass, and lacquers. While most dining rooms share a simple layout of table and chairs, Coleman proposes that it is the shapes and finishes that make a dining space unique. In this case "it is the finish on the table that makes it interesting, the mixing of metal with the wood on the chairs, the elliptical shape of the servers in two different sizes, and the two different white wall coverings…" The main dining pieces are by Dakota Jackson, the light fixture is an intertwined metal piece by Brand En Van Egmond, from Miami. The sheer window fabric, by Bergamo, has a playfulness to it because it crunches up when touched.

Coleman believes this room is high-end "because of the quality of materials and finishes and the obscurity of the furniture." According to Coleman, high-end design requires "a certain clientele that gives you the luxury to create spaces for them that have almost no limits."

Photography by Floto & Warner

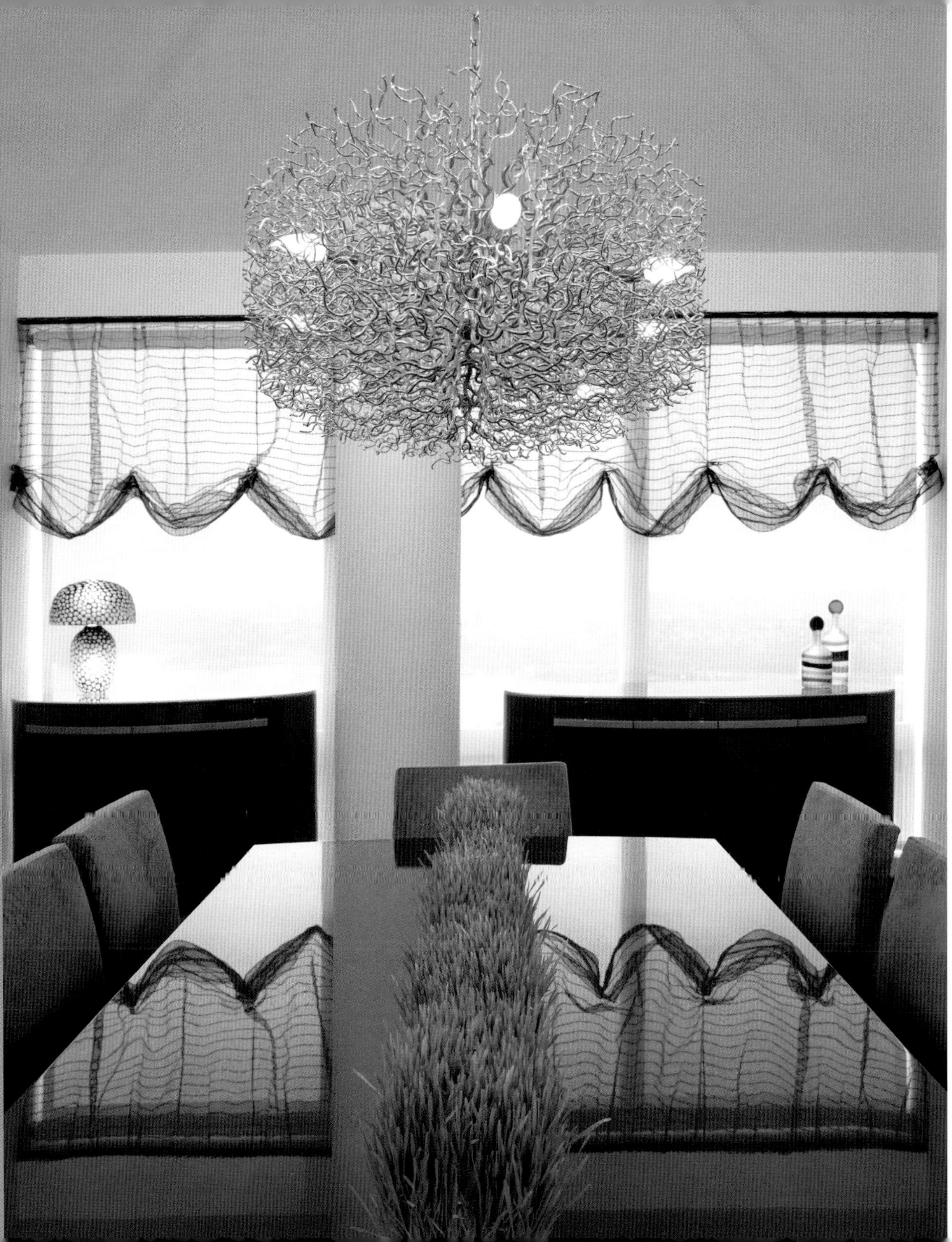

JOHN BARMAN, INC.

Inspired by the architecture of the building, John Barman wanted to carry the 1960s and 1970s aesthetic into the interior of his space. "Whatever I am doing, I do it all the way. I don't water things down. Whatever style I am doing, I do it completely."

True to his word, Barman jazzed up the inside of his apartment with furniture, colors, and art with the "hard edge modern look." He selected bright red and yellow because he finds it "vibrant and exciting and fun to go into the room" in those colors. The furniture included an Angela Adams red carpet, bright yellow Milo Baughman chairs around a Saarinen table, and Mies van der Rohe Barcelona chairs. The dining room boasts a painting of the same period by Jack Goldstein and a stainless steel table designed by Barman.

Barman's design is high-end because of the caliber of the work that went into preparing the space before any furniture was added, including the paint job, the lighting, the drapery, and the poured concrete floors. Not only did he make the space "correct," but his design is high-end because of his "usage of materials that are unexpected, materials that people might not think are durable," such as fur, and that he "worked with a complete look."

Photography by Billy Cunningham

MARTIN RAFFONE
INTERIOR DESIGN

When Martin Raffone's client requested his home be like a gallery space for his art collection, Raffone knew better than to create the typical, cold, all-white gallery interior. The space he created has "an impression of an all white environment, but there is a richness to it."

Raffone selected furniture that felt natural and let the art pop. "Everything looked sort of bleached out, like it had been lying in the desert or on the beach for a hundred years and all the natural color came out of it." The oak floors were bleached to get all the color out, as with the antique spruce on the mantel. The result was a streamlined, "creamy and ethereal" space with no real color palette. "It is a white space, but every material had a story about how it came to lose its color identity." In other areas where he used non-white materials, such as blackened metal or stone, "even though the materials are not white per se, the rawness and naturalness of them have a whiteness to them conceptually; they are almost raw – there is nothing to them except what you see." The streamlined furnishings in natural shades of brown do not interfere with the artwork.

Raffone says of this project, "It is a high-end idea, not every client in the world could understand what I was trying to do here." Specifically, the quality of attention paid to every surface, such as the paneling, was a labor of love. "There is a rarification to the way things are detailed" that can only be found in high-end design, where the client has the budget and willingness to let the designer lavish attention on every detail.

Photography by Ake E:son Lindman

RICHARD TRIMBLE & ASSOCIATES

Richard Trimble's clients challenged him to create a dining room that successfully melded the couple's very different tastes – contemporary vs. traditional – and personalities – creative vs. delineated. Trimble claimed, "One of the best compliments you can have is that the clients say the room expresses them." Inspired by the mix of influences, Trimble created a warm, welcoming dining room with a look that can be interpreted as a good match for a variety of styles.

Trimble chose to work with shades of celadon green, because it is "a current but classic color." The decorative Chinese chairs were traditional looking, but he recovered them in a more contemporary, Donghia fabric. Trimble incorporated an antique Chinese altar table as a server to balance the contemporary dining chairs. While he chose a Venetian chandelier for the ceiling, he lightened the floorboards to their natural color for a fresher look. The dining table was from the 1960s, but Trimble had it refinished in a more contemporary finish. The drapery was full and elegant, but not fussy.

Trimble's room is high-end because it had a simple, sophisticated look to it. "It is not necessarily the most expensive materials, but it is the mixture of what we put together in the room that gives it a sophisticated look."

Photography by Dan Piassick

AMANDA NISBET DESIGN, INC.

Amanda Nisbet aspired to design a happy, elegant, family-friendly home with a lot of color. She selected blazing yellow to make the place cheery and chic; a win for a New York apartment that did not get too much light.

Nisbet said of her startlingly beautiful yellow drapery vignette, "I wanted to make a big impression." She balanced the other side of the room with a yellow club chair, and added striped pieces and a plush velvet sofa. She stained the floor a chocolaty brown instead of laying an expensive rug, making the place inviting for either children or grown-ups. "I want everyone to enjoy it, not feel like they are in the wrong room."

Nisbet's design is high-end because it "works as a whole." Despite her affection for color and her notorious skill at applying it, she claimed, "I don't want it to look like I had been there. I want the room to be a reflection of the client."

Photography by William Geddes

NORTHBROOK DESIGN

Katherine North was inspired to create a spacious interior in a small space that was also bright and timeless.

After gutting this bathroom, she played with color, mirror, and glass to energize different planes and give the space life. She chose the Catalano sink because she wanted something floating in the corner, making the space feel weightless. The white, textured, handmade Heath Ceramics tiles added a "timeless" element to the bath, while the bright, orange walls kept the space fresh and warm. The glass at the end of the tub, the mirrors, and the skylight all contribute to the room's spacious feel. "It is not forced, it looks natural. It is just what you need, it is not over the top."

North's design is high-end because, while there are not many elements in the room, each item was carefully selected or custom built, and demanded a high budget. "It looks simple and straightforward, but that comes from a lot of thought and effort," she added. "The more spare a room is, the more well thought out it has to be."

Photography by Lanola Kathleen Stone

MATTHEW PATRICK SMYTH, INC.

Matthew Smyth recognized that he used his apartment mostly for evening entertaining, so he aspired to create a space that glowed and felt welcoming and striking at night. He was inspired by a red Italian vase he found on a trip and had a painter cover the walls in a similar color. "I always wanted to have red walls," he explained, adding, "it is an exciting, fun color. It has a definite statement and looks good in all seasons."

With red as his lead, Smyth set about adding items to the room that would suit the high contrast background and his personality. "I wanted things that were clean and designed, not too sterile, and everything with a masculine bent to it." He found the mirror over the sofa in a smaller version and had it recreated in a larger proportion. He chose striped fabric for the chair to highlight the shape of it, to add a vertical element, and to keep the room from getting too dark. The table from Cassina with a curved front was an easy, non-aggressive shape to have. "When I pick out objects, furniture, it is all about the silhouette." He enjoyed the texture of the large olive jar sitting on a smooth, rectangular, metal shape, next to the campaign-style chair. The pieces come to life in contrast to the red walls. "When picking a strong color – you can do it but you must make the rest of the room go with it. You have to just go for it."

Smyth speaks about his work: "In this case – it is not about money, it is about accumulation of everything I've learned and studied over the years. It is all about me. It is personal. It is edited. All of these things are what makes high-end design something that is not thrown together; attention was paid to it. It does not have to be expensive, but it has to be purposeful."

Photography by Peter Margonelli

"I wish I could go through life with these walls behind me."

CAROL KIPLING

Kipling was inspired "to bring the outdoors in" to create a serene, soft environment fit for a male client. She took cues for the inside by taking colors and textures from the patioscape outside.

Kipling repeated the color of the tree bark in the color of the sofa, the color of the sage green plantings in the carpet, and the turquoise flowers in the accessories. Kipling wanted to respect the mid-century architecture of the house, but also soften it, because she felt mid-century can look cold. "This type of design, being very boxy, with its use of glass and open beams, can leave a space feeling very harsh," she said. Kipling focused on adding curves, soft materials, a lot of texture, and stayed away from stark white walls. Finally, by designing each piece of furniture to fit her tall client, she achieved lasting, "ergonomically correct comfort." She extended the seat of the sofa and chairs to best fit her client's long legs and back, details that enabled him to enjoy the space more.

Kipling's design is high-end because she successfully wove the outside and inside together in a "luxurious, earthy, and comfortable" palette.

Photography by Thomas A. Heinz

ROBERT COUTURIER
& ASSOCIATES

Robert Couturier's living room is both a private space as well as a space for clients. He treats it like a set full of objects he adores, changing them around often. As he said, "I come back late at night, and start moving the furniture around." Couturier believes that houses are a direct reflection of who we are when we design them, so naturally they must change over time. Couturier is clearly comfortable handling and changing furniture, being well schooled in the laws of proportion and balance, he confidently rearranges pieces with ease to suit his mood.

Couturier said, "I use a great variation of furniture, I don't want to be homogeneous in terms of style." He cautioned you do not want "too much one way so clients think you can only do this or that." He kept the colors fairly neutral, left out moldings and cornices so he could move the furniture around easily, and focused on the walls and windows. He hung heavy drapes because "In New York City, you want to be able to isolate yourself from the cold and fog, and when it is bright and sunny you want to open the windows." The checkerboard design on one wall was inspired from a palace in Japan. Couturier takes a European approach to ensure there are plenty of places for guests to sit down. "In America, most people at cocktail parties stand up, they don't sit. In Europe you arrive somewhere and people immediately flop down."

"You have to allow yourself to make mistakes. It takes trying things together to get it right."

Couturier's design is high-end because it took a lot of effort and "a certain form of study." In contrast to mass design of today, "where everybody has the same thing, and you get tired of it," Couturier believes that the individuality of high-end design is what is exciting. "Something that is done with effort always appears more interesting." Similar to how he approached his own living room, "As long as you like things, they work together, to a degree," because designers are capable of putting elements together in a space and making them work. "It comes instinctively."

Photography by Bruce Buck

HEATHER WELLS LTD.

Heather Wells aspired to create a traditional, beachy woman's sitting room. She selected slate blue as the perfect color to create a mood that was "restful and peaceful, feminine, but not frilly."

Building her design from this color, Wells doused the walls in the color and added a blue linen pattern on the ceiling. She painted the molding white "to achieve the illusion of crown molding," and added linen drapes to give the room a "light, airy feeling." A few silver accessories provided a touch of feminine glitz, and she found ways "to combine traditional form in a clean line way," such as layering an Oriental rug on sea grass. Wells said of her design that she was "playing to the Bostonian," and that it is key to "play to a certain audience in your own style."

Wells claims high-end design is "paying attention to all the little things," and it is, simply, "the way things feel."

Photography by Eric Roth

EKB INTERIORS

Eileen Kathryn Boyd used the beautiful wood grid pattern on the floor as a base for her design. "I am very aware of geometry and scale to get the proportions right," she claimed. She also wanted to make a statement in color, so she chose a confident palette of pink and green.

Looking for some unique ways to add detail to her design, Boyd looked to fashion. "There are so many clues in couture details." The draperies have dressmaking frogs and an interchangeable sash attached from the top. She added a green hem-like border to the wingback chairs, and a soft skirt to the pink slipper chairs. "It was off the runway and into the home," she said.

Boyd's design is high-end because the colors and proportions interact in perfect harmony, like a great outfit. "People walk in and say 'this feels good to me,' they don't know why, but it hits a certain note." Boyd's design is based on classic forms, but the individual pieces have been tweaked or updated in some way, providing visual delight and discovery.

Photography by Mark Samu

STEF-ALBERT STUDIOS LLC

Stef Albert wanted to create a room full of light, comfort, and warmth, at the same time, with a reference to the ocean. Covering the seating in white with blue accents evoked those elements. As he said, "It's a very instinctive thing, but then I do adjusting."

Albert painted the walls a soft cameo color to provide a soothing background for the white. The sisal rug added warmth and casualness to the space, and the neutral tones "brought the outside in." Albert always designs his rooms keeping in mind what they are like at night. To him, the tone of lampshades, the fireplace, and candles can make a big difference in how a room is perceived. At night, the white of this space is warm and inviting. Should the client ever want a break from the white, they can simply change the slipcovers on the chairs.

For Albert, "Quality is very important – I always use the best quality materials my clients can handle." He added that high-end design is "the skill of how to use different genres and put them together so the space works, and going the extra mile with special finishes and things that could be done for a client that they don't necessarily know for themselves."

Photography by Kelly Marshall

PLUSH HOME

Nina Petronzio wanted to create a bedroom that was "Pleasing to look at, timeless, elegant, but not contrived." She chose a combination of colors that would be neither too feminine nor too masculine.

Petronzio said, "You want a room to look like it happened over a period of time, not put together at once. It's more personal." Along that vein, she purposefully mixed a variety of pieces in one room. The upholstered headboard, the mahogany dresser, and the red and white upholstered chair work together, but they don't feel as if they all came together at one time. She added the cow print bench because, in every project, she looks to add "that one little extra thing."

Petronzio's design is high-end because most of the pieces in the space were custom-designed by her for the space and her unusual mix of fabrics. "High-end design exists when a space exudes elegance, quality, and fine attention to details." She added that when designing furniture she works closely with craftsmen for the purpose of creating furnishings "worthy of becoming family heirlooms."

Photography by Steven Ho

DIANE PAPARO ASSOCIATES

Prodded by her client, Diane Paparo was inspired to pick the color palette for this project by the color of the client's dog. The result – a sunny, warm, camel color dominated the scheme, balanced by chocolate, pumpkin, and teal.

The striking ceiling height encouraged Paparo to design the bed herself, ensuring the result was of the appropriate scale. The chaise lounge was new, but next to it she placed a sleek, modern antique. "When people think old, they think old and dusty and ornate, but that is not necessarily the case." A signature move for Paparo, the "his and her" sides of the bed were complimentary, but not identical, like two people in a marriage. She accessorized the space with a careful eye to the grand scale of the room, as she explained, "People often misjudge scale. Sometimes all the accessories from one project need to grouped together as a single accessory in another project."

Photography by Philip Jensen-Carter

"High-end design is the result that could be successfully achieved by someone who is well educated and experienced in design and decoration and strives to achieve the results using the highest quality materials and craftsmanship, and may not necessarily include extremely expensive pieces, but is able to select among those things that have design integrity." **– Alan Tanksley**

FIVE:
ARCHITECTURE & SPACE

LAURA BOHN DESIGN ASSOCIATES

Laura Bohn moved into an old bank building, and as she had the floors polished up, a warm brown came through and started "talking" to her. Inspired by the color of the existing floor, Bohn developed the rest of the space from there. "The oak went with the concrete floor and from there to animal skin rug, to all the toffee and brown tones, and leathers. It is a high-end rustic look."

Bohn designed the sofas with backs and sides in leather and cushions in mohair to "mix luxurious and toughness" and for "the opportunity to use more than one material." Bohn plays a lot of materials against each other, "sometimes pairing five different fabrics in the same color." The cowhide in the center of the floor was the perfect complement to an odd-sized room and the glass table on top offered an element of elegance and fragility in contrast to the heavy concrete and wood. Bohn added, "It is a rough space. It is detailed, but it is rough."

Bohn's design is high-end because it is highly detailed. "It is so detailed – even the sheet rock does not meet the ceiling to provide a clean edge. Every tile is laid out; it is complicated stuff. And, it was expensive." Yet in general, Bohn does not limit her perspective on high-end to expensive pieces. "I am one of those people who loves finding things that are cheap and fabulous. I like anything I can find that costs two dollars. I am crazy about anything green, anything manmade, recycled, anything plastic, anything I haven't seen before – it is fun. I love to mix those things in."

Photography by Cynthia Van Elk

DAVID HOWELL DESIGN

David Howell, in collaboration with client Debra la Chance, wanted to "respond to the inherent character of the raw envelope." This loft, perched on top of a building with substantial views, felt to him like an urban tree house.

In order to create the sense of a tree house, Howell chose to "minimize the visual interference in the interior, but also make it feel rich and cozy." He worked with a dark floor as a foundation for a light and playful mix of elements. He added light-colored contemporary furniture, and an upholstered orange chair for punctual contrast. The walls of the entry leading up to this space Howell painted chocolate brown, making the living room feel more rectilinear and able to carry the eye outside.

Howell believes "high design starts at space management and making the arrangement of the space feel luxurious." He carefully planned the seating areas to feel spacious, even in economized space. He designed the exquisite millwork for the fireplace, making that whole area of the room "feel like a volume, and those volumes begin to relate to each other, creating a sense of warmth."

Howell's work and his relationship with the client exemplifies that high-end design is not achieved by big budgets, but rather by passionate people who believe in the design process who are able to, "make rooms behave and feel as they should."

Photography by David Joseph

"The scale is not grand, but the space has grandeur about it."

BETTY WASSERMAN
ART & INTERIORS, LTD.

Betty Wasserman envisioned a modern, formal living room, a tailored space where "one might sit upright and have a glass of champagne in an evening dress," as opposed to lounging in front of a TV. The vision suited this 7,000 square foot Manhattan townhouse, where having space for a designated formal entertaining room is a luxury itself.

Wasserman's challenge was that the space had a thirty-foot ceiling, and enough seating for one-and-a-half areas. To transform this vertical, boxy space into an elegant, intimate one, Wasserman added horizontal and curved lines. She selected a Zimmer & Rhode silk fabric with horizontal stripes, chose Andree Putman curved furniture from Pucci, and installed a rich wood with a subtle horizontal grain above the slate fireplace. To keep eyes from drifting upward and to avoid clumsy lamps and wires, she installed in the ceiling a "constellation of urchin custom lighting" by Helen Gifford, providing a fantastic, organic form floating above the main seating area. Behind this area, Wasserman installed the client's Steinway macassar wood piano, successfully filling the extra space with a formal entertaining element. Wasser

man attests that "high-end design is well-planned, well thought-out, having the ability to do custom things, and having free range as far as lighting, floor finishes, cabinetry, and custom furniture. If you can't do those things then it is not high-end." She applied these elements and her refined level of expertise to every detail in the room.

Photography by Eric Laignel

"The room tells you what you should be doing in there."

ZK INTERIORS LTD.

The modern architecture and fantastic views in this space inspired Cara Zolot & Elizabeth Kohn, founders of ZK Interiors, to keep the interior design simple and let the windows dominate. They wanted to present the feeling that you are floating up in the sky among the clouds.

Zolot and Kohn chose a neutral palette and pieces with simple, straight lines. The custom, contemporary sectional sofa frames the corner of the main seating area, anchoring the space. They liked the Arne Jacobson Egg chairs in the window not only because they swivel and are functional to utilize the views, but also because they symbolize a modern aesthetic. "We get inspired by beautiful pieces we find along the way, and then the rest of the room unfolds." A light fixture, found at John Salibello, was a perfect fit for the space with its modern profile and translucent quality. Kohn and Zolot designed the dining table, a Lucite base with a glass top, "so you can see straight through to the views."

Zolot and Kohn share the view that high-end design requires an appreciation for the arts – line, form, function – and the ability to integrate them all into one.

Photography by Matthu Placek

APPLEGATE TRAN INTERIORS

Inspired by the concept of a "New York loft, but more sophisticated than a grungy New York loft look," Vernon Applegate turned to a monochromatic palette and elements that would reflect the San Francisco city lights.

Applegate used mostly cool tones to minimize the variety of colors and allow the views to prevail. He chose the floor and area rug to be similar in color so the space would flow continuously. The contemporary sofas, covered in a grey-blue fabric, were chosen for their low height relative to the window. The oversized chair in grey leather is architectural – it has a noticeable mass, but it also blends in with the room. The choice for glass and other reflective materials for cabinets and doors maximized the reflection of city lights, contributing to the urban feel. Applegate chose a dark garnet color for the ceiling to provide warmth and a touch of contrast against all the cool tones.

The design is high-end because even without a lot of furniture or color, the quality of the finishes and details are enough to excite and engage the eye. As Applegate said, "Even though a lot of the pieces are very simple, it is how they are stitched, how the fabric meets the frame of the furnishing… there are so few pieces in there every little piece is noticeable."

Photography by David Duncan Livingston

JANSON GOLDSTEIN LLP ARCHITECTURE & INTERIOR DESIGN

Mark Janson was inspired to weave old and new together in this Park Avenue study/dining room for his aesthetically contemporary clients. His approach was to use "traditional materials and colors, but the language of the architecture would be modern."

Instead of framing the fireplace with travertine marble in the traditional way, Janson set a large piece of travertine flush with the sheetrock wall to act as a backdrop for the items in the room and to provide visual interest. Similarly, he chose French modern chairs with clean, contemporary lines, but covered them in fabrics chosen because they looked like they "had a history." For bookcases, Janson skipped the traditional wooden variety and installed sleek, metal cases to provide a twist on the classic Park Avenue study. The result was a space comfortable with itself and for its clients. "There is a real casualness to the space and comfort. The absence of formality is purposeful for who the client is."

Janson's design is high-end because in addition to the high-level materials and craftsmanship used in the space, "for this project what is special is the time that was invested by us, the clients and contractor, to make everything exquisite, right, and per the client's request."

Photography by Michael Weschler

C.M. RABINOVITCH/ ARCHITECTS

Charles Rabinovitch aspired to design a quiet retreat within an urban environment. Working within only the small confines of a studio apartment, Rabinovitch was able to achieve a sense of spaciousness and serenity.

Key to Rabinovitch's design was to hide most of the client's personal effects and visually divide the space. He integrated a tremendous amount of storage with sleek built-in cabinetry in the living space and natural finish anodized aluminum and sand-blasted verde silver granite cabinetry in the kitchen. Rabinovitch created depth with special cues such as elevating the sleeping area and changing the floor surfaces. A chaise in pumpkin orange punched the space with color.

Rabinovitch's design is high-end because his smart use of space and materials. As he said, "Things that appear to be almost non-events, meaning they just disappear into the space, are actually the result of carefully executed design and fabrication." Rabinovitch added, "Clearly at times high-end is linked to high budget, but I would like to think it is not always the case," but rather, he hoped high-end referred to "a high level of thought and execution which goes into the producing of a residential space."

Photography by Andrea Rabinovitch

COLVIN DESIGN

Danny Colvin wanted to design "a great party space for two to two hundred people." Using a simple, neutral, crisp, modern palette, he intended this New York loft to be "not too fancy," but rather "serene and natural."

Colvin developed his neutral palette using all one wood, one stone, one paint color – with splashes of color only from cushions or artwork. He left the meat-packing loft's structural columns in their original state with holes where they hung meat hooks and scratches of rope to provide contrast with everything new that was sleek. He added a glass wall by the entry foyer to create a space for private conversation during large events. He chose Baker armless chair-and-a-halves and a sixteen foot long bench so there would be plenty of flexible seating during parties. The dining table and chairs were the perfect match for the place because, not only did they offer plenty of space to either dine or serve food, but also the two tones of wood picked up on the other simple wood tones in the room.

Colvin's space is high-end because of the craft applied to simple materials to make them appear extremely elegant. As he said, "All the maple is exquisitely done and perfectly sequenced, it is the simplest, least expensive wood you can get – but treated with such care and intent that it seems much more expensive than it is."

Photography by Elizabeth Felicella

JAMES RIXNER

James Rixner strove to design a clean, classic, contemporary space without the usual clichés, using elegant finishes to accentuate the space. Inspired by his client's need for space, Rixner's concept was "to blow the space wide open, and to keep it luxuriously open everywhere you look".

After knocking out most of the walls, Rixner set about defining functional areas with furniture and area rugs. He applied tone-on-tones of celadon throughout. The Brazilian cherry, wide-plank floors provide a uniquely rich setting for the graceful, contemporary furniture. "The drama of the space is not only the space, but also the incredible windows." The windows deserved the perfect shade of wool sateen drapery, but when Rixner could not find what he was looking for, he had it made. He used the same customized approach to completing the staircase – when the right shade of wood and metal were not readily available for purchase he had the stairs constructed on site.

Rixner's careful eye designed, corrected, and beautified every aspect of this loft. "Simple, contemporary spaces are almost harder to execute, you can't hide anything anywhere. The structural work has to be clean and perfect." He added, "high-end is paying attention to detail that is not readily available over the counter, and it is an approach that everything can be customized to the clients' needs and wishes."

Photography by Jay Rosenblatt

LESLIE C. BAHR DESIGN

Inspired by the architecture of this old firehouse she renovated, Leslie Bahr kept thinking about the concept of ladders. "There is something about the metaphor of a ladder that I really liked," she said.

Building upon the theme of ladders and connections, Bahr wanted to create intimacy with the furnishings in a luxurious, classical modern motif. She purchased a 1940s French sofa from Allan Moss, and she placed it among other Edward Wormly pieces. She covered the upholstery in simple fabrics, but then contrasted them with legs of high sheen. "I approach things with an understated relationship of materials that comes through contrast or sheen." Bahr wanted to soften the contemporary look. "Too often in contemporary what's done is to use very modern furnishings, and that all becomes too hard edged looking for me."

Bahr's design is high-end because of her talent in combining pieces in a way that complements the architecture. As she said, "High-end design is about the relationship between things; it's a way of perceiving space, a subtle but elegant use of materials, that isn't overwhelming."

Photography by Cesar Rubio

BASIL WALTER ARCHITECTS

Architect Basil Walter, inspired by the importance of this foyer, "the point of arrival in the house" developed a balanced, classic modern interior. In collaboration with Eric Cohler, he aimed to make the space feel "meditative… because of the manner in which we think about every detail, but have the overall effect of the space be about the architecture and the light, but not about trying to create a statement that would in any way have the wow factor of the room overwhelm the details of history and nuance."

Walter wrapped the staircase around the elevator shaft, giving a sense that the stair is "flowing down into the room," with space on either side. "When we do townhouses, we look to create space where you can perceive the light from front to back – it creates a tremendous sense of space." Working with designer Eric Cohler, the idea was "to create a golden glow to reflect the brassy gold character of the chairs and chandelier." Walter added, "we wanted the chairs and table to be counterpoints to the wall. The effect is that the room is very rich in color but is not overwhelmed by the color." Similarly, he added, "We coffered the ceiling because we wanted to create a space that had some note of classicism to it but wasn't defined by classicism," and "we juxtaposed frosted glass and the wooden banister, crown moldings, and colored walls, all to provide a modern interplay with history." One of Walter's talents is to keep the elements in careful balance.

Walter believes that high-end design projects can be distinguished by all the time spent considering every aspect. He said, "There is no simple formula to make it happen."

Photography by Bilyana Dimitrova

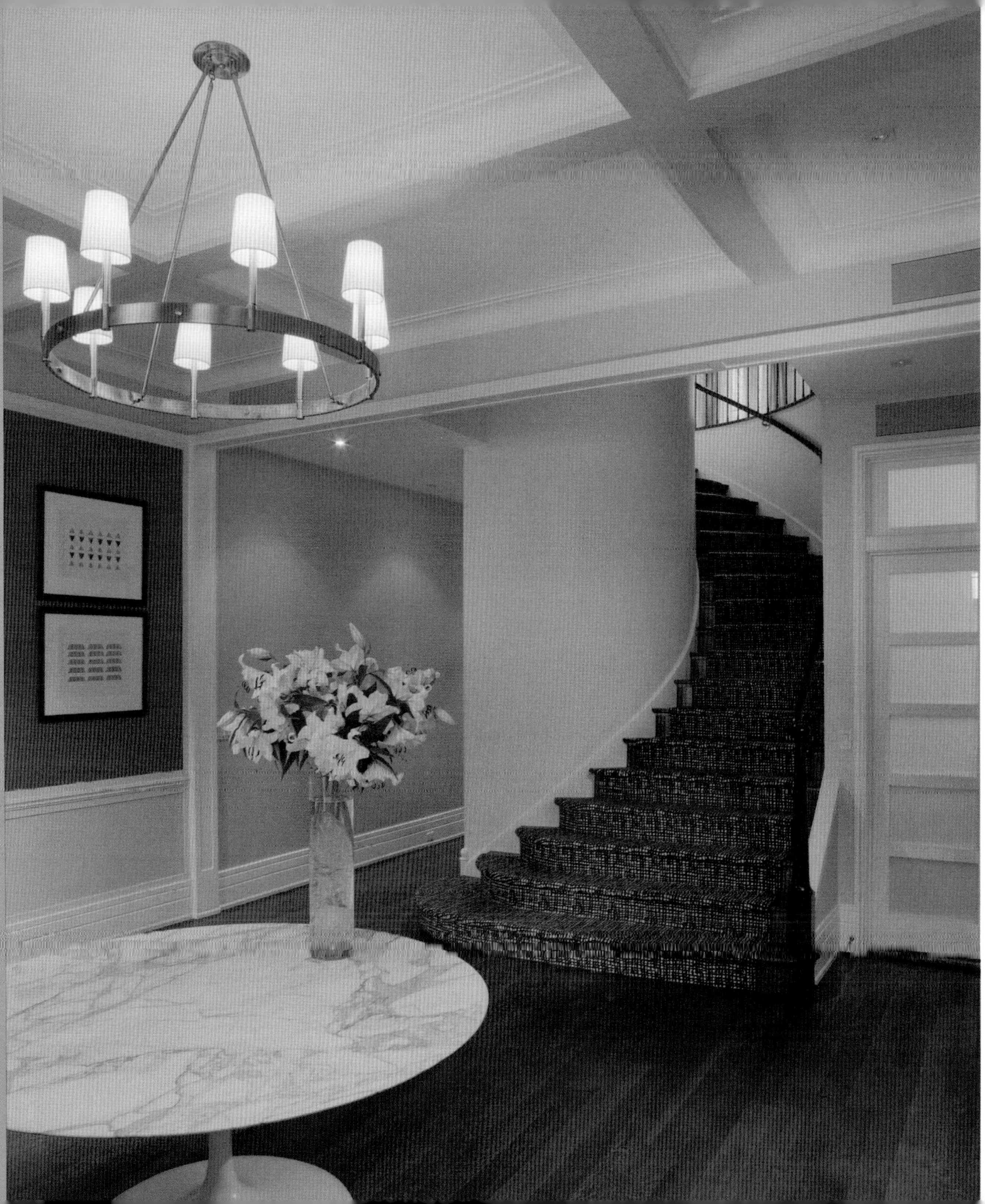

VALERIE PASQUIOU
INTERIORS & DESIGN, INC.

Valerie Pasquiou was inspired to give this architecturally traditional living/dining space a contemporary, warm ambiance. Working with furniture styled with simple lines and an array of organic pieces, Pasquiou transformed the space into an inviting retreat.

Pasquiou started with earth tones and then added brighter colors to them, giving the space a bit of visual excitement. Pasquiou designed the sofas, armchairs, and ottoman to be loungy, casual, and comfortable, and then integrated some more organic pieces such as a raw steel and exotic wood console by Japanache, and a soft wool rug by Denis Colomb. She added the B&B Italia standing mirror for reflection and to increase the size of the room.

Pasquiou's design is high-end because of her comfortable juxtaposition of simple organic materials and fabrics, and the warmth created by carefully crafted lighting. She definded high-end dsign as "simplicity, warmth, elegance, timelessness." She added, "I don't believe in trends or extreme minimalism in living environments. Trends die quickly."

Photography by Erica Lennard

JON ANDERSEN
DESIGN SERVICE

When designing the parlor of a Victorian South End row house, Jon Andersen kept in mind what a friend told him once: "I have never been in a Victorian townhouse parlor that didn't remind me of a bordello or a funeral home." Andersen promised himself that his house would feel like neither.

Although Andersen had a bent for contemporary design, in restoring this house he lovingly added back the 12-inch molding around the windows as it would have been. In the process, he thickened and insulated the wall, adding traditional shutter pockets and luscious, formal, silk drapery. "It's fun to use the historic envelope, and allow it to be historic, and then have a dialog with the old and something new and serene." He then added contemporary furniture, such as B&B Italia white chaises, a simple sisal rug, a clean Donghia Bellagio sofa, and contemporary artwork, such as the bubble mirror. "Being in New England, it's fun to mix in contemporary furniture in these antique houses."

Andersen's design is high-end because of the high level of refinement of the objects. "If you didn't know the cost of the things, there is a subtle quality that comes through." He added, "It doesn't hit you over the head, there are no shiny, glossy objects, yet it has a quiet richness that infuses the place. That is the optimal feeling."

Photography by Dave Henderson

"When you are talking about a 150 year old house, you don't own it. It's a historic structure. You just live there for a little while."

GREG LANZA DESIGN

Greg Lanza was inspired to make the architecture shine in this house because the soaring cathedral ceilings, large stonework fireplace, and prevalence of the light and views from outside demanded it.

Desiring to emphasize the architecture over color, Lanza chose a natural palette of creams and linens for the interior. He defined each area of the large, open room with area rugs. Building on a subtle nautical theme, Lanza sewed a grommet and sailing rope piping detail on the backs of the dining chairs. Lanza chose the highest quality comfortable fabrics for the furniture, including Summer Hill chenilles and a variety of custom colored, highest-grade fabrics.

Lanza's design is high-end because of the appropriate use of space, light, and color. "It is quality of the materials, the suitability of history, and the interpretation of what you are trying to achieve," that makes a space high-end. He added, the key to excellent design is, "Getting the design nailed on the head by knowing history and the appropriate use of materials."

Photography by Tim Ebert

THOMAS JAYNE STUDIO, INC.

Thomas Jayne was inspired by the architecture of this old New York brownstone – both the existing details, such as intricate crown moldings and door casings, and the new features, such as the grand staircase, "the ornament of the house."

Taking cues from the architecture, which was redesigned with Basil Walter Architects, Jayne turned to vintage pieces. He started with finding a rug for the living room and from there added furniture that had a bit of "gravitas" to it, including tufted club chairs, an intricately carved coffee table, and luxurious drapes with gold tape detail. "Old things make us understand new things, we need both." He added, "I try hard never to make things so old fashioned they are not inhabitable." Jayne aspired to keep the house feeling fresh, spacious, and a "place with history but not overwhelmed or repressed by it."

Jayne's design was high-end because the furniture and accessories were handpicked to enhance the history and architecture of the building, rendering a cohesive, intelligent design. As Jayne said, "It was a great recycling project, things were not picked from a catalog."

Photography by William Waldron

S.L.C. INTERIORS, INC.

"The beautiful, natural setting of Nantucket, which drove the architecture, pushed us to use a quiet interior color palette," said Susanne Csongor of S.L.C. Interiors. Inspired by the seaside views, Csongor kept the interiors of this space simple, with more variation in texture than color.

She used "bone, sand, and driftwood colors" on the upholstery to keep from "challenging" the views, and placed wingback chairs in front of the fireplace to reference a traditional seating arrangement with two chairs in front of the fire. The artwork, a commissioned piece with Nantucket subject matter, is the visual focal point of the room.

Susanne attested it is "the quality of the materials, beautifully woven textiles and case goods" that make this space high-end. In addition, "There is an understanding of architecture, principles of good design, proportion, color, light, balance. We understand things such as how a piece of fabric is woven, and all of that orchestrates all the other elements to a higher level."

Photography by Durston Saylor

ROGER HIRSCH ARCHITECT & TOCAR, INC.

Designer Christina Sullivan explained that she and her partner Susan Bednar Long of Tocar "wanted to extract our clients' aesthetic and bring to life a new environment for them." Architect Roger Hirsch, of Roger Hirsch Architect, added that the new environment he and his associate, Myriam Corti, were to develop needed to transform the boxy apartment into an open loft. While they removed existing rooms and structures, they also had to "give them back functionality," and thus focused on using every inch of the place to its maximum.

The team collaborated to create something warm, but also fresh, new, and not overbearing. They focused on selecting and building unique pieces made from rich materials. They chose a dining table by Jerome Abel Seguin because of its heavy presence and texture. Tocar designed the chairs made from teak and apple green French tapestry from J. Robert Scott. The rich floor color derived from Ardex mixed with Benjamin Moore paint, and the sophisticated, modernized Murphy bed, dropped from a Macassar ebony structure veiled by sheaths of Rogers & Goffigon gauze.

Tocar and Hirsch's design was high-end because "everything was designed – every nook and cranny" – every detail from the custom-cut floor planks, to the drawers lined with orange ultra suede, to the cashmere-lined, pop-up desk units that include corkboards. Sullivan stated high-end design was "anything that is designed by instinct, which is created through a vision and relates to the client." She added, "It has to be sophisticated but subdued at the same time." Hirsch attested, "For some people high-end might mean very expensive materials and fixtures, for us as architects, it means the client is willing to invest enough money in the space to make it really individual and customized for them."

Photography by Michael Moran

"In this era of 'fast fashion', where trends change so frequently, we get accustomed to 'disposable design'. High-end design doesn't follow trends. It sets them, and, if done properly, is timeless."
– **Will Wick**

"High-end design is a refinement of tastes, a careful selection of beautiful objects."
– **Matthew Patrick Smyth**

INDEX & CREDITS

ARCHITECTS & INTERIOR DESIGNERS

2Michaels Design
360 Central Park West, Suite 16H
New York, NY 10025
212-662-5358
www.2michaelsdesign.com
info@2michaelsdesign.com

Alan Tanksley, Inc.
114 East 32nd Street, Suite 1406
New York, NY 10016
212-481-8454
www.alantanksley.com
ati@alantanksley.com

Alice Wiley Associates LLC
Showplace Square West
550 Fifteenth Street, Suite 30
San Francisco, CA 94103
415-861-6700
www.alicewiley.com
info@alicewiley.com

Amanda Nisbet Design, Inc.
1326 Madison Avenue, Suite 64
New York, NY 10128
212-860-9133
www.amandanisbetdesign.com
info@amandanisbetdesign.com

Angela Free Interior Design
San Francisco, CA
415-885-4193
www.angelafreedesign.com
angela@angelafreedesign.com

Ann Getty & Associates
Ann Getty House Collection
P.O. Box 471026
San Francisco, CA 94147
866-343-3890
www.anngetty.com
inquires@anngetty.com

Applegate Tran Interiors
Sobel Design Building
680 Eight Street, Suite 260
San Francisco, CA 94103
415-487-1241
www.applegatetran.com
vernon@applegatetran.com;
    gioi@applegatetran.com

Ashley Roi Jenkins Design
1580 Lombard Street, Suite 2
San Francisco, CA 94123
415-409-1689
www.arjdesign.com

inquire@arjdesign.com

Barbara Ostrom Associates
One International Boulevard, Suite 209
Mahwah, NJ 07495-0009
212-807-8030

Basil Walter Architects
611 Broadway, Suite 311
New York, NY 10012
212-505-1955
www.basilwalter.com
info@basilwalter.com

Betty Wasserman Art & Interiors, Ltd.
212-352-8476
www.bettywasserman.com
info@bettywasserman.com

Carol Kipling
6710 Melrose Avenue
Los Angeles, CA 90038
323-934-4080
www.carolkipling.com
info@carolkipling.com

Christopher Coleman Interior Design
55 Washington Street, Suite 707
Brooklyn, NY 11201
718-222-8984
www.ccinteriordesign.com
info@ccinteriordesign.com

Clodagh
670 Broadway, 4th Floor
New York, NY 10012
212-780-5300
www.clodagh.com
info@clodagh.com

C.M. Rabinovitch/Architects
4525 Henry Hudson Parkway
Riverdale, NY 10471
212-989-3554
archrabin@aol.com

Coddington Design
Melanie Coddington
San Francisco, CA
415-285-2821
www.coddingtondesign.com
melanie@coddingtondesign.com

Colvin Design
Danny Colvin
345 West 13th Street
New York, NY 10014
917-903-1265 (c)
212-727-1262
www.colvindesign.com
danny@colvindesign.com

Constantin Gorges Inc.
646-234-5686
www.constantingorges.com
constantin@constantingorges.com

Dana Nicholson Studio Inc.
515 Broadway
New York, NY 10012
212-941-6834
www.dananicholson.com
nicholsonstudio@aol.com

Darren Henault Interiors, Inc.
216 West 18th Street, 11th Floor
New York, NY 10011
212-677-5699
www.darrenhenault.com
info@darrenhenault.com

David Desmond, Inc.
1360 North Crescent Height Blvd.
Los Angeles, CA 90046-4503
323-650-0492
www.daviddesmond.com
ddesmond@daviddesmond.com

David Howell Design
200 Park Avenue South, Suite 1518
New York, NY 10003
212-477-7700
www.davidhowell.net
david@davidhowell.net

Diane Paparo Associates
344 East 59th Street
New York, NY 10022
866-473-2224
www.paparo.com
diane@paparo.com

Edward Lobrano Interior Design Inc.
155 East 56th Street, 3rd Floor
New York, NY 10022
212-751-0550
www.edwardlobrano.com
edward@edwardlobrano.com

EKB Interiors
Eileen Kathryn Boyd
251 Main Street
Huntington, NY 11743
631-427-6400
www.ekbinteriors.com
eileen@ekbinteriors.com

Eric Cohler Design
872 Madison Avenue
New York, NY 10021
212-737-8600
www.ericcohler.com
ecohler@ericcohler.com

De La Torre Design Studio
Ernest De La Torre
526 West 26th Street, Suite 6AA
New York, NY 10001
212-243-5202
www.delatorredesign.com
ernest@delatorredesign.com

Drake Design Associates
Jamie Drake
315 East 62nd Street, 5th Floor
New York, NY 10021
212-754-3099
www.drakedesignassociates.com
jamiedrake@drakedesignassociates.com

Geoffrey De Sousa
De Sousa Hughes
2 Henry Street, Suite 220
San Francisco, CA 94103
415-626-6883
www.desousahughes.com
Geoffrey@desousahughes.com

Geoffrey Bradfield Inc.
116 East 61st Street
New York, NY 10021
212-758-1773
www.geoffreybradfield.com
gnbradfield@aol.com

Glenn Gissler Design
36 East 22nd Street
New York, NY 10010
212-228-9880
www.glenngisslerdesign.com
info@glenngisslerdesign.com

Grant K. Gibson Interior Design
3792 Sacramento Street
San Francisco, CA 94118
415-939-0243
www.grantkgibson.com
grant@grantkgibson.com

Greg Lanza Design
75 Highland Road
Glen Cove, NY 11542
516-656-9848
lanzaid@aol.com
www.greglanzainteriors.com

Hayslip Design Associates, Inc.
Sherry Hayslip
2604 Fairmount Street
Dallas, TX 75201
214-871-9106
www.hayslipdesign.com
info@hayslipdesign.com

Heather Wells Ltd.

359 Boylston Street #2
Boston, MA 02116
617-437-7077
333 West Hubbard Street, #2E
Chicago, IL 60610
312-464-0077
www.hgwltd.com
info@hgwltd.com

James Rixner
121 Morton Street
New York, NY 10014
212-206-7439
www.jamesrixner.com
jr@jamesrixner.com

Janson Goldstein LLP Architecture & Interior Design
180 Varick Street
New York, NY 10014
212-691-1611
www.jansongoldstein.com
hg@jansongoldstein.com

Jean Alan
2134 North Damen
Chicago, IL 60647
773-278-2345
www.jeanalanchicago.com
jean@jeanalanchicago.com

The Jeffrey Design Group
Noel Jeffrey
215 East 58th Street
New York, NY 10022
212-935-7775
www.noeljeffrey.com
info@noeljeffrey.com

Jeffers Design Group
Jay Jeffers
550 15th Street
San Francisco, CA 94103
415-934-8088
11601 Wilshire Blvd., Ste 500
Los Angeles, CA 90025
310-235-1423
www.jeffersdesigngroup.com
jay@jeffersdesigngroup.com

John Barman, Inc.
Design and Decoration
500 Park Avenue
New York, NY 10022
212-838-9443
www.johnbarman.com
info@johnbarman.com

Jon Andersen Design Service
625 Tremont Street
Boston, MA 02118

617-536-0004
www.jads.biz
jon@jads.biz

Jones Footer Margeotes Partners
      Architecture & Interior Design
Kerry Delrose
245 Mill Street
Greenwich, CT 06830
203-531-1588
www.jfmp.com
info@jfmp.com

Kari Whitman Interiors
P.O. Box 2357
Beverly Hills, CA 90213
310-652-8684
www.kariwhitmaninteriors.com
kwinteriors@aol.com

Kathryn Waltzer Interior Design
310-890-0712
www.kathrynwaltzer.com
info@kathrynwaltzer.com

Kathryn Scott Design Studio Ltd.
126 Pierrepont Street
Brooklyn Heights, NY 11201
718-935-0425
www.kathrynscott.com
kscott@kathrynscott.com

Kenneth Hockin Interiors
Old Chelsea Station, Box 1117
New York, NY 10011
212-647-1955
www.kennethhockininteriors.com
contact@kennethhockininteriors.com

Laura Bohn Design Associates
30 West 26th Street
New York, NY 10010
212-645-3636
www.lbda.com
info@lbda.com

Leslie C. Bahr Design
10 Carmel Street
San Francisco, CA 94117
415-664-1678
www.lesliecbahrdesign.com
lcbdesign@hotmail.com

Madeline Gelis Inc
222 East Pearson, #204
Chicago, IL 60611
312-943-7464
www.madelinegelis.com
madelinegelisinc@sbcglobal.net

Martha Angus Inc.

1017 Bush Street
San Francisco, CA 94109
415-931-8060
www.marthaangus.com
marthaangus@marthaangus.com

Martin Raffone interior design
247 Centre Street, 7th Floor
New York, NY 10013
212-243-2027
www.martinraffone.com
info@martinraffone.com

Matthew Patrick Smyth, Inc.
12 West 57th Street, Suite 704
New York, NY 10019
212-333-5353
www.matthewsmyth.com
smythinc@aol.com

Maureen Wilson Footer & Associates
212-207-3400
info@mwfooterdesign.com

Matthews Studio
Nestor Matthews
1099 23rd Street, #4
San Francisco, CA 94107
415-550-6700
www.matthewsstudio.com
info@matthewsstudio.com

Northbrook Design
Katherine Northbrook
10 Arkansas, Studio F
San Francisco, CA 94107
415-934-8400
www.northbrookdesign.com
info@northbrookdesign.com

Philip J. Meyer Ltd.
1005 Bush Street
San Francisco, CA 94109
415-673-6984
www.philipjmeyerltd.com
info@philipjmeyerltd.com

Plush Home
Nina Petronzio
8323 Melrose Avenue
West Hollywood, CA 90069
323-852-1912
www.plushhome.com
info@plushhome.com

Richard Trimble & Associates
3617 Fairmount Street
Dallas, TX 75219
214-526-5200
trimble_associates@sbcglobal.net

Robert Couturier & Associates
69 Mercer Street
New York, NY 10012
212-463-7177
www.robertcouturier.com
robert@robertcouturier.com

Robert Passal Inc.
36 West 22nd Street
New York, NY 10010
212-242-5508
www.robertpassal.com
robert@robertpassal.com

Roger Hirsch Architect, LLC
91 Crosby Street
New York, NY 10012
212-219-2609
www.rogerhirsch.com
roger@rogerhirsch.com

Ruby, Inc.Bella Zakarian Mancini
41 Union Square West, No. 1036
New York, NY 10003
212-741-3380
www.rubylife.com
bella@rubylife.com

Scott Sanders L.L.C.
524 Broadway, Suite 400A
New York, NY 10012
212-343-8298
www.scottsandersllc.com
info@scottsandersllc.com

Shane Reilly Inc.
244 Madison Avenue, #218
New York, NY 10016
2370 Market St., #142
San Francisco, CA 94114
415-602-4454
www.shanereilly.com
shane@shanereilly.com

Sherrill Canet Interiors, Ltd.
3 East 66th Street, Suite 4B
New York, NY 10021
212-396-1194
www.sherrillcanetinteriors.com
sherrill.canet@sherrillcanet.com

SKB Architecture and Design
Nestor Santa-Cruz
1818 N Street, NW, Suite 510
Washington, D.C. 20036
202-332-2434
www.skbarch.com
hhotopp@skbarch.com

S.L.C Interiors, Inc.

Susanne Csongor
264 Bay Road
Hamilton, MA 01982
978-468-4330
www.slcinteriors.com
susanne@slcinteriors.com

Stef-Albert Studios LLC
212-203-9483
www.stefalbertstudios.com
stef@stefalbertstudios.com

Thrasher Design Company
Jeffrey Thrasher – Principal
P.O. Box 398 506
Miami Beach, Florida 33239
305 538 9442
thrasherdesignco@aol.com

Thomas Jayne Studio, Inc.
136 East 57th Street, #1704
New York, NY 10022
212-838-9080
www.thomasjaynestudio.com
tjayne@thomasjaynestudio.com

Tocar Interior Design
Susan Bednar Long & Christina Sullivan
165 Madison Avenue #500
New York, NY 10016
212-779-0037
www.tocardesign.com
info@tocardesign.com

Todd Klein, Inc.
27 West 24th Street, Suite 802
New York, NY 10010
212-414-0001
www.toddklein.com
todd@toddklein.com

Tucker & Marks, Inc.
Suzanne Tucker
Ghirardelli Square
900 North Point Street, Suite B-201
San Francisco, CA 94109
415-931-3352
www.tuckerandmarks.com
info@tuckerandmarks.com

Valerie Pasquiou Interiors & Design, Inc.
1855 Industrial Street, #608
Los Angeles, CA 90021
213-402-1500
www.vpinteriors.com
valerie@vpinteriors.com

Wheeler Design Group
Marion Wheeler
531 Vermont Street

San Francisco, CA 94107
415-863-7766
www.wheelerdg.com
info@wheelerdg.com

William McIntosh Design
216 West 18th Street, Suite 1002
New York, NY 10011
212 807 8030
www.williammcintoshdesign.com
info@williammcintoshdesign.com

Wick Design Group
Will Wick
360 Langton Street, Suite 100
San Francisco, CA 94103
415-437-0125
www.wickdesigngroup.com
info@wickdesigngroup.com

The Wiseman Group Design, Inc.
Paul Wiseman
301 Pennsylvania Avenue
San Francisco, CA 94107
415-282-2880
www.wisemangroup.com
contact@wisemangroup.com

Your Space Interiors
Charles De Lisle
43 Seventh Street
San Francisco, CA 94103
415-565-6767
www.your-space.com
charles@ysinteriors.com

Zeff Design
Mark Zeff
515 West 20th Street, #4W
New York, NY 10011
212-580-7090
www.zeffdesign.com
abarr@zeffdesign.com

ZK Interiors Ltd.
Elizabeth Kohn & Cara Zolot
1 Union Square West, #511
New York, NY 10003
212-924-6667
www.zkinteriors.com
elizabeth@zkinteriors.com;
      cara@zkinteriors.com

PHOTOGRAPHERS

Adrian Wilson
212-729-7077
Adrian@interiorphotography.net
www.interiorphotography.net

189

Ake E:son Lindman
+46 8 34 35 80
Ake.eson@fotograf-lindman.se
www.fotograf-lindman.se

Billy Cunningham Photography
212-929-6313
Bcham44@earthlink.net
www.billycunninghamphotography.com

Bilyana Dimitrova Photography
347.693.4314
bilyana@bdphotography.com
www.bdphotography.com

Bruce Buck Photography
212-645-1022
bwbuck@frontiermet.com
bruce@brucebuck.com

Cesar Rubio Photography
415-550-6369
cr@cesarrubio.com
www.cesarrubio.com

Christopher Covey Photography
805-648-3067
Covey4x5@aol.com

Cynthia Van Elk
917-488-4420
www.cynthiavanelk.com
Cynthia@cynthiavanelk.com

Dan Piassick Photography
214-688-0554
dan@piassick.com
www.piassick.com

Daniel Aubry Photography
212-414-0014
Daniel1aubry@aol.com
www.aubryphoto.com

Henderson Studio
Dave Henderson
617-842-0878
www.hendersonstudio.com
dave@hendersonstudio.com

David Duncan Livingston
415-383-0898
www.davidduncanlivingston.com
david@davidduncanlivingston.com

David Joseph Photography
917-690-6000
davejojo@aol.com
www.davidjosephphotography.com

Dennis Krukonski
212-860-0912

Dominique Vorillon
323-660-5883

Douglas Hill Photography
323-660-0681
odouglas@pacbell.net
www.doughill.com

Durston Saylor
212-779-3901
thaxton@aol.com

Elizabeth Felicella
efelicella@nyc.rr.com

Eric Laignel
917-204-4338
ericlaignel@hotmail.com

Eric Piasecki Photography
917-940-4139
ericpiasecki@earthlink.net
www.ericpiasecki.com

Eric Striffler Photography
516-220-6707
www.striffler.com
eric3@striffler.com

Eric Roth Photography
978-887-1975
Sabrina@ericrothphoto.com
www.ericrothphoto.com

Erica Lennard
310-721-6057

Floto & Warner
212-947-2281
contact@flotowarner.com
www.flotowarner.com

Francis Smith
646-831-0264
francis@francissmith.net
www.francissmith.net

Frank Veteran
212-749-5544
nareten@mac.com

Gordon Beall Photography
301-581-0486
gb@gordonbeall.com
www.gordonbeallphotography.com

Gross & Daley
212-679-4606
gdphoto@att.net

Jay Rosenblatt Photography & Visual
    Communications, Inc.
973-731-1616
jayrosez@earthlink.net
www.jayrosenblatt.com

Smith Photography Studio L.L.C.
John Smith
214-744-0477
john@smithstudio.com
www.smithstudio.com

Johnny Miller Photography
212-344-0025
jm@johnnt-miller.com

Kelly Bugden
212-677-4743

Ken Gutmaker Photography
415-282-2600
www.kengutmaker.com
ken@kengutmaker.com

Lanola Kathleen Stone Photography
917-502-9519
Stone@lanolakathleen.com
www.lanolakathleen.com

Laurie Lambrecht Photography
212-534-0188
laurie@lambrecht.com

Lydia Gould Bessler
212-741-3458

Samu Studios
Mark Samu
212-754-0415/518-581-7026
msamu@samustudios.com
www.samustudios.com

Margot Hartford Photography
415-821-0441
margot@margothartford.com
www.margothartford.com

Matthew Millman Photography
415-577-3200
matthew@matthewmillman.com
www.matthewmillman.com

Matthu Placek
212-253-1953
matth@matthuplacek.com
www.matthuplacek.com

Melissa Castro Photography
415-846-9121
Melissa@melissacastro.com
www.melissacastro.com

Michael Moran Photography, Inc.
212-334-4543
Michael@moranstudio.com
www.moranstudio.com

Michael Robinson Photography
312-451-1221
Michael@mrobinsonphoto.com
www.mrobinsonphoto.com

Michael Weschler Photography
212.315.2875
917.570.4085 Cell
mw@michaelweschler.com
www.michaelweschler.com

Mick Hales Photography
518-672-0014
mhales@halesart.com
www.halesart.com

Nancy Elizabeth Hill
203-431-7655

Pat Miller Photography
516-364-4096
www.patmillerphotography.com
pmphoto@optonline.net

Peter Margonelli
212-941-0381

Peter Murdock Photography
212-255-4001
www.petermurdock.com
info@petermurdock.com

Philip Jensen-Carter
914-557-1739
pjcpixler@optonline.net

Phillip Ennis Photography
914-234-9574
phillip@phillip-ennis.com
www.phillip-ennis.com

Steven Barker
212-226-2505
917-767-8841

Steven Ho
323-852-1912
steven@plushhome.com

Tim Street-Porter Studio
323-874-4278
www.timstreet-porter.com

Thomas A. Heinz
847-328-6532
tanarch@earthlink.net

Tom Sibley Photography
917-923-8875
info@tomsibley.com
www.tomsibley.com

Will Brewster Photography
406-587-5619
www.willbrewster.com
brewsterphoto@earthlink.net

William Geddes Studio
212-524-0852
www.williamgeddes.com
William@williamgeddes.com

William Waldron
212-505-3193
ww@williamwaldron.com
www.williamwaldron.com

Wouter Van dur Tol
+310 20 530 6000

FABRIC CREDITS

Donghia - Ebb and Flow in Pale
Blue - #20017-02

Pollack - Giorgio Sheet in
Parchment - 9088/02

Innovations - Lizard in Bone - 2102

Donghia - Grasscloth II in
Hammock - 20001-20

Wolf Gordon - Mr. Lucky Gaffer -
WG 4166091

Robert Crowder & Company -
Corduroy Stria - RC-8541

Henry Calvin Fabrics #2494

INDEX

US $44.95

ISBN: 0-7643-2499-3

192